Metaphors of Ed Tech

Issues in Distance Education
SERIES EDITOR: *George Veletsianos*

METAPHORS
OF ED TECH

Martin Weller

◊ AU PRESS

Published by AU Press, Athabasca University
1 University Drive, Athabasca, AB T9S 3A3
https://doi.org/10.15215/aupress/9781771993500.01

Cover design by Bryan Mathers, Visual Thinkery
Interior art by Bryan Mathers, copyright © The Open University, licensed under a
Creative Commons Attribution licence.
Printed and bound in Canada

Library and Archives Canada Cataloguing in Publication
Title: Metaphors of ed tech / Martin Weller.
Names: Weller, Martin, author.
Series: Issues in distance education series.
Description: Series statement: Issues in distance education series | Includes
bibliographical references.
Identifiers: Canadiana (print) 20220254311 | Canadiana (ebook) 20220254354 |
ISBN 9781771993500 (softcover) | ISBN 9781771993517 (PDF) | ISBN 9781771993524 (EPUB)
Subjects: LCSH: Educational technology.
Classification: LCC LB1028.3 .W42 2022 | DDC 371.33—dc23

We also acknowledge the financial assistance provided by the Government of Alberta
through the Alberta Media Fund.

To Maren, who listened patiently to random metaphors.

CONTENTS

Metaphors of Ed Tech

The Role of Metaphor

I was lucky enough to be in Florence, Italy, once. I had just given a keynote on digital scholarship and then set off to view some of the artistic treasures for which the city is rightly famous. At the top of my list was seeing the bronze statue of Perseus holding aloft the head of Medusa in the Piazza della Signoria. The statue, cast by Benvenuto Cellini in 1554, is a visceral depiction of the mythological slaying of the Medusa, famous for its realism and gory representation of blood. I spent some time looking at it, and because I was simultaneously reviewing the keynote that I had given, I began to make connections between the two. The casting process, I knew from my studies in art history, was recounted by Cellini as some mythical life-giving act. Medusa is an ancient symbol of misogyny, and in this I saw echoes of how new technology can reinforce existing power structures. It was obvious, I thought, but why had no one written about the Perseus–educational technology analogy previously? Later that night in my hotel room I blogged some thoughts on this. I knew by then that it was rather a stretched metaphor, but it was enjoyable to play with and write about the connections. And tenuous though it might be, the analogy still made some valid points, to my mind, and in a novel manner.

This more playful aspect of thinking and writing about educational technology (ed tech) is the primary reason that I have maintained a blog since 2006. It provides me with a space in which to explore and be creative that is not appropriate in most of the formal requirements of my job and the outputs produced. I often use metaphors on my blog (its tag line is "Martin Weller's blog on open education, digital scholarship & over-stretched metaphors") and have a preference for those far removed from ed tech itself. Anything can be a metaphor (although not necessarily a good one), and it is this liberty that I think is often missing in our relationship with technology in education. The freedom to play with ideas, and to explore new ways of thinking, critiquing, deploying, and analyzing ed tech provided by metaphors, is much needed if we are to develop a better appreciation of its possibilities, implications, and limitations. I would also argue that, given how much our relationship with ed tech is embedded in very pragmatic issues, metaphor provides a welcome outlet to creativity for those whose daily practice is linked to it. This case for metaphor is what I hope this book goes some way toward making.

In this book, I propose a number of different metaphors that relate to aspects of educational technology. At the time of writing, we are still enduring the COVID-19 pandemic, which suddenly forced nearly all educational institutions to engage in some form of online learning. Often it has been a rather rushed version of the classroom model by hosting online sessions in Zoom or some other synchronous tool. However, as the longer-term implications of the pandemic are considered, many schools and higher education institutions (HEIs) are planning to use a blended model that incorporates aspects of online delivery and face-to-face learning. For many institutions and educators, educational technology has suddenly taken centre stage in their strategies. The criticisms of online education that proliferated during what became known as "the online pivot" revealed a considerable lack of understanding about how educational technology can be deployed effectively, what the real issues are in developing meaningful online education, and what the dangers are of simply accepting the rhetoric on technology. We will look at the online pivot in more detail, but what the period revealed was a lack of appropriate mental models for people to think about online education. The face-to-face approach of the lecture dominates so much of the thinking in higher education that anything outside it is usually discussed only in terms of a deficit model—how does it differ from the traditional lecture?

This is one prominent example of why I believe that offering a range of metaphors for positive and negative aspects of ed tech is worth developing. Metaphor provides a means (not the only method, I should stress) of considering ed tech that does not rely on a direct comparison with the existing model. I should also add that I believe it is an endeavour worth pursuing, and worth your time reading about, partly because thinking of metaphors and their application is an interesting activity and, if you are like me, quite an engaging thing to do. But more significantly it is because ed tech now, particularly since the pandemic, plays a central role in education. Ed tech is a multi-billion-dollar industry, and the role of companies and technology will have an influence on how education is realized in the coming years. The future of education and change within the sector are nearly always couched in terms of responding to the challenges presented by technology (e.g., Rigg, 2014), developing skills in students to function in a digital society and economy (e.g., Learning Wales, 2018), and implementing technology or associated business models (e.g., Christensen, et al., 2009). How ed tech is framed and presented is often manufactured to suit the needs of those with vested interests. For example, the near-ubiquitous theory of disruption is commonly cited, but it is almost entirely without credit or applicability in education. It does, however, suit vendors of new software to shape the conversation as one of revolution that requires radical change and the admission of new entrants into the sector. Understanding and thinking about ed tech—its implications, issues, and context—will be essential in shaping how it is used. Metaphors are a means of achieving this, and in this introduction I want to set out why I think they are important and therefore why they can be significant in our relationship with ed tech.

Metaphors and Education

The pioneering work of Lakoff and Johnson (1980) was largely responsible for moving metaphors into a central position in understanding how people make sense of, and operate within, the world. They argued that, rather than being a tool of "the poetic imagination," metaphors in fact are central to how people think, and our "ordinary conceptual system . . . is fundamentally metaphorical in nature" (p. 3). Because metaphors are so embedded in our language and models of thinking, we often do not even recognize something as a metaphor. Lakoff and Johnson (p. 5) provide the example of "argument is war": we say that "your claims are indefensible" or that "I demolished their argument." This shapes how we think about an argument—as something with an opponent, that can be won, in which there are strategies and rhetorical weapons. Metaphors shape how we act and live in this view. Sfard (1998, p. 4) contends that metaphors are "the most primitive, most elusive, and yet amazingly informative objects of analysis." That is, they shape our language and thinking in fundamental ways but often remain hidden until coaxed into view.

The definition of "metaphor" varies according to domain, so practitioners in linguistics, psychology, literature, and anthropology might use the term slightly differently. Metaphors are a non-literal use of language; for example, when we say that "my dog flew across the garden to chase the squirrel," we do not mean that the dog literally grew wings and flew. Metaphors can be seen as a super-category of all such uses of language, including analogy and simile. In this book, I focus on the use of metaphors as an educational tool rather than on their use in shaping our relationships with the world. In this context, metaphors act as analogies that allow us to map from a familiar domain in order to understand an unfamiliar domain. This is referred to as structure mapping, "the central idea [of which] . . . is that an analogy is a mapping of knowledge from one domain (the base) into another (the target), which conveys that a system of relations that holds among the base objects also holds among the target objects" (Gentner, 1989, p. 201).

This is a tool often used in education, for example the (rather erroneous but still useful) analogy of the structure of the atom and the solar system. In this instance, the base, or source, domain is the solar system, and the structure of the atom is the target domain. This allows relationships between elements to map across, so the sun is like the nucleus, and smaller electrons orbit around it in fixed paths like the planets. Some elements we map across from the source domain to the target domain, and others we do not (e.g., an atom does not need to have the same number of electrons as planets in the solar system). A good metaphor will help people not only to understand new concepts but also to make predictions about them, but an incorrect mapping of certain elements can similarly lead to poor conclusions.

Metaphor has been proposed as one of the main methods by which we come to understand a topic. McCloskey (2005) suggests that there are two dominant ways by which people come to understand a topic—by metaphor or through narrative (or models and histories)—and that different fields tend to be dominated by one mode; for instance, metaphors dominate physics, whereas narratives dominate biology. In 2020, I published a book, *25 Years of Ed Tech*, that could be considered complementary to this book, although this is very much a stand-alone piece. Both books can be seen, though, as essentially seeking to answer the same question: "How can we better understand ed tech?" The former book can be seen as the narrative response to that question, whereas this one can be seen as the metaphorical response. Both approaches are valid but work better in particular contexts or for different audiences.

From the research on metaphors, we can extract two significant elements relevant to this book. First, they are fundamental in shaping our interactions with the world; second, they can be used to understand a new domain. This makes metaphors powerful tools in many areas, not least of which is politics, framing how we view both social policy problems and their solutions (Schön, 1993). For instance, if a politician talks about crime as a disease, then it carries with it a number of connotations from the source domain (e.g., crime can spread like an infection, but there is a cure, and so on). By shaping the argument in such a manner, politicians are in a position to present themselves, or their policies, as the solution. A different framing of the problem, for example crime as monster, carries a different set of connotations. Thibodeau et al. (2009, p. 814) tested this hypothesis by presenting a problem in terms of these two metaphors; according to which one they were presented with, people were likely to propose different solutions: "When crime was compared to a virus, participants were more likely to suggest reforming the social environment of the infected community. When crime was compared to a predator, participants were more likely to suggest attacking the problem head on—hiring more police officers and building jails." A politician with a platform of building more jails will likely frame the problem of crime in terms of a predator or monster that needs to be controlled. The proposed solution looks more favourable than a rival proposition about investments in local communities. Similarly, shaping technology in terms of certain metaphors makes some solutions more "obvious" or suitable than others.

Metaphors, then, are a powerful means of understanding or explaining topics. Lukeš (2019) proposes three uses of metaphor in explanation.

- Metaphor as invitation. When learners are new to a subject, a metaphor can provide a route in, such as the atom and solar system example, but Lukeš argues that this type of use "does not help understanding. It just provides emotional support along the arduous journey towards that understanding." That is, a deeper understanding of the target domain is required, and too often people stop at this stage.

- Metaphor as instrument. This involves exploring both target and domain and the connection between them and finding where the metaphor does not apply. This leads to a deeper understanding and a useful mental model.

- Metaphor as catalyst. This requires a deeper knowledge of the target domain, and here the metaphor allows manipulation of both elements, and the learner will make independent judgments and predictions.

Using this classification, the metaphors in this book aim to act as instruments, hopefully with the potential for being catalysts if readers pursue them further. My intention is to provide metaphors of sufficient richness to allow exploration, which will include considering when the metaphor does not apply, what its limits are, and a possible alternative.

Turning to the use of metaphors in ed tech itself, in 2000 Nardi and O'Day argued for the significance of metaphor in relation to how society discusses, uses, and is shaped by technology: "Metaphors matter. People who see technology as a tool see themselves controlling it. People who see technology as a system see themselves caught up inside it. We see technology as part of an ecology, surrounded by a dense network of relationships in local environments" (p. 27). Gozzi similarly argued in 1999 that metaphors were a key factor in understanding new technology and in fact were increasing in use as a consequence. For example, phrases such as "the information superhighway" and "computer virus" reveal how metaphors helped to shape our understanding of this unknown domain. Nardi and O'Day (2000) proposed four main metaphors: tool, text, system, and ecology. Mason (2018) deployed discourse analysis to extend this list by examining the literature of educational technology research in the social sciences. He found five categories of metaphor:

- manual labour—ed tech as a tool;

- construction/building—ed tech as an aid in scaffolding and constructing knowledge;

- mechanism—ed tech as a machine;

- biological life/agent—ed tech as an ecosystem or evolution; and

- journey—ed tech as a "journey leading toward greater use of new technologies which will yield positive consequences for teaching and learning" (p. 545).

There will be examples of these metaphors in many articles and reports on different forms of technology. The use of such metaphors is perfectly valid, and no single metaphor is necessarily better than another. But it is important to realize how each one frames the view of technology, how it is used, what it should do, and what its benefits and drawbacks are. These metaphors are often used without realizing that they are in fact metaphors—they seem to be "common sense"—or acknowledging their power in shaping our concepts of technology. It is not just that we can or should use metaphors in thinking creatively about technology but also that we do so all the time, and by acknowledging them we can, as Schön (1993) argues, become critically aware of them.

Education itself is couched deeply in terms of metaphors. Wilson (1995) proposes four fundamental metaphors for learning: the classroom, product delivery, system definitions, and process definitions. Depending on which model a software developer adheres to will influence the type of educational technology developed or how it is deployed in an institution. If you see learning as product delivery, then the sort of technology favoured will be focused on organizing and managing content that can be delivered to learners. If, however, the dominant metaphor is one of process, then the technology will support different stages in a learning process. Similarly, Botha (2009) proposes nine uses of metaphor in education, including how we shape educational policy (e.g., student as consumer), how we view the learning process (e.g., learner as sponge), how we frame teachers (e.g., teacher as guide), and how we talk about education in society. Metaphors, then, are key to how we think about, implement, practise, and evaluate education and thus the role that we see for technology within it. Sfard (1998) suggests a distinction between two basic learning metaphors—acquisition and participation. Acquisition is characterized by knowledge and concepts constructed by the learner, with the teacher involved in activities such as delivering content or facilitating learning. Participation involves ideas of apprenticeship and communities of practice in which learning is "not considered separately from the context within which it takes place" (p. 6). Sfard contends that we need both metaphors to develop meaningful learning, and the idea that metaphors need not be exclusive, or that one is superior to another, is important to keep in mind.

This work on metaphors highlights the motivation for this book and why the consideration of metaphors in ed tech is worthy of attention. Since I will focus on metaphors of educational technology, it is worth defining what the term "educational technology" refers to in this respect. It has a long history and can include any technology used in an educational context, from chalk and blackboard to virtual reality. It can also include related technology, for instance surveillance software. There is a joke about the only educational technology known to work is the school bus, which indicates that the definition can be broad indeed. In this book, though, my focus is on digital, networked technology used within higher education. Educational technology in schools is an important topic but closely allied with national or regional policies and directives. Some of the metaphors in this book will be applicable at this level also, but the tertiary education sector is the scope of most of the chapters.

I propose three reasons why metaphors in ed tech are worth exploring.

1. Educational technology is a relatively new field compared with the longer tradition of face-to-face, classroom teaching. Its implications, impacts, possibilities, and problems are aspects that researchers are still trying to comprehend. Metaphors therefore provide a useful means of understanding this new field.

2. The use of metaphors shapes how ed tech is deployed. As with the example of politicians, the control of language is important. If ed tech vendors describe technological change as an "avalanche," for instance (Barber et al., 2013), then it seems to be substantial, unavoidable, and catastrophic (at least if nothing is changed). It is important, then, to appreciate when metaphors are being used and for what purposes. Therefore, I will explore some of the metaphors that shape ed tech and why they can often be damaging or limiting to the implementation of technology to the benefit of learners.

3. Metaphors allow us to reason in a different manner about technology. Using a metaphor, particularly an unusual one, we can see different aspects of something, which can challenge our original thinking. Through the use of metaphors, we can think creatively when considering ed tech. I would argue that much of our relationship with ed tech is quotidian and pragmatic. A practical approach to technology is fundamental, but there is also room for imagination, creativity, and even playfulness when we consider it.

About This Book

My intention in this book is to explore each of these three elements through a number of different metaphors. The preceding discussion of metaphors is brief but hopefully sufficient enough to provide an adequate overview. I could devote the whole book to an exploration of the research on metaphors for technology, but that is not my aim. This is not primarily a book *about* metaphors, or metaphorical reasoning, but a book *of* metaphors. They have usually arisen from my blog (blog.edtechie.net) over the past decade or so, where I often use metaphors to explore aspects of ed tech. Metaphors are an appropriate tool to use in writing a blog since they are distinct and allow for some playful thinking, which suits the medium. I have continued that approach here, so many of the metaphors in this book are rather stretched or intended lightly. I have deliberately avoided political metaphors where the source domain (e.g., Brexit) carries so many connotations that it overshadows any mapping to a target domain. It is also true that some of the metaphors here run contrary to the mapping process set out above in that the source domain might be as unfamiliar as the target domain. For example, when I use the purpose of a Welsh castle to examine the reasons for investment in ed tech, it requires a certain level of initial explanation. This is an example of an interactive metaphor, in which it is a matter not of mapping and substitution between domains but of interaction between them. Botha (2009, p. 432) claims that "in a metaphor an interaction takes place between two semantic fields. This leads to the creation of a novel meaning." It is this creation of novel meaning and understanding that is the intention of the metaphors in this book. The second type of metaphor that I explore is currently used for aspects of ed tech, and by examining such metaphors I explore their connotations and, as with the "crime" metaphor, how they are used to shape solutions.

I hope that the metaphors in this book offer something in terms of how we approach and think about educational technology and our relationship with it. Some of these you will undoubtedly find more fruitful than others, but each chapter is largely independent, so you can skip to a different metaphor if you prefer. In examining a broad range of metaphors, I am aware that I could be guilty of dilettantism, cultural appropriation, or a version of what Primo Levi (1986) called "literary lechery." I have therefore tried to draw from areas that I know well for the metaphors; for example, you will find a reasonable number of references to Wales since it is where I live. Yet the metaphors end up being rather Western or Global North–centric. I am not sure how to square this circle, but I hope that, where I have used metaphors outside my immediate experience (e.g., some borrow from aspects of religion), I have done so appropriately and that, even if the metaphors are not sufficiently global in their perspective, their range is sufficient to create interest for most readers or at least to suggest ones that might be more applicable in their own context. I hope to have demonstrated that there is no boundary to what constitutes a useful metaphor and that this freedom is one way of reshaping our relationship with technology.

I also created a tool similarly playful in tone that generates metaphors for ed tech (http://metaphor.edtechie.net/). Using this method of thinking, which might seem to be trivial on the surface, provides a route to exploring and discussing the application of technology that often brings serious issues into focus. My aim in this book is to draw attention to the benefits and dangers of metaphorical approaches to ed tech and thereby to give us a better understanding of what we want from technology and how best to realize it.

The book is divided into chapters that group metaphors of a similar nature together. They all relate to some aspect of ed tech, although what qualifies as educational technology is given a loose definition. It is probably worth briefly addressing some of the terms before we continue since many of them overlap, have varying definitions, and are sometimes used by particular groups in specific ways.

Distance learning: this term refers to education in which educator and learner are not physically co-located. The UK Open University and similar institutions were founded as distance-learning institutions with the specific intention of removing distance as a barrier to education. Although it is usually delivered online, this is not necessarily the case, and it can deploy a number of methods, including online, correspondence, and broadcast media.

Online learning: this term applies when the primary method of learning is realized via the internet. It often overlaps with distance learning but highlights the aspect of technology. As noted, distance learning can utilize methods that are not online (e.g., printed materials mailed to students), and online learning can involve students who are co-located (e.g., in drop-in centres). The term "online learning" is largely synonymous with the term "elearning," more popular in the late 1990s.

Blended learning: this term covers a broad range of possibilities and emphasizes the use of different elements. It can refer to a blend of technologies and media, for example printed books, online forums, computer simulations, and podcasts. It refers more commonly to teaching that combines face-to-face and online learning, for example weekly face-to-face tutorials combined with online learning completed remotely. A rise in blended learning approaches is likely to be one of the long-term impacts of the COVID-19 online pivot as HEIs develop solutions that combine the best of both elements.

Hybrid learning: this term is often used synonymously with blended learning, although it can refer to a distinct approach. Whereas blended learning combines online and face-to-face learning for students, hybrid learning refers to the combination of online and face-to-face learning at the same time, so some students will be in a classroom, laboratory, or lecture hall while others will be watching and interacting online. This approach puts pressure on the educator to create appropriate learning experiences so that the online element is not a lesser option than the face-to-face element.

Educational technology: this is the term (abbreviated as ed tech) that I have chosen to encompass all of these aspects. It encompasses all applications of technology to education, but as discussed earlier it is usually meant to address digital, networked technology. I have opted to use this term partly because of its broad coverage and partly because it is a widely used term that people generally have an instinctive appreciation of but that is not too tied down in academic camps around specific applications.

Digital scholarship: in the book *The Digital Scholar* (Weller, 2011), I argued that the term "digital scholarship" provides a convenient short-hand in contrast to traditional, "analogue" forms of scholarship but that "digital" is only one aspect of a trilogy. It is best viewed as the change in scholarly practice that occurs at the intersection of digital, networked, and open approaches. I use the term in this book to highlight the changes in the practices of academics, educators, and researchers. The term "open practice," which encompasses academic activities based upon online sharing, is not quite synonymous but related.

The chapters in this book explore different aspects of all of these terms. The chapters are as follows.

- "An Example of Metaphorical Thinking": using visual metaphors created for the multidisciplinary program at the UK Open University, how metaphors can reveal different aspects of education is highlighted to provide an example of its application.

- "Thinking about Ed Tech": setting the basis for the book, metaphors that help us to think about ed tech in general and its role in higher education are explored.

- "Ed Tech as an Undiscipline": following from the previous chapter, there are some metaphors that examine the concept of thinking about ed tech as a discipline or field of research.

- "Specific Ed Tech": the metaphors in this chapter narrow the focus from the broader field of ed tech to specific technologies such as massive open online courses (MOOCs) and learning analytics.

- "Ed Tech Criticism": the business of educational technology is one in which metaphors are often used to frame an argument. In this chapter, some of these metaphors, such as "Uber for education," are examined and their implications considered.

- "Open Practice": aspects of openness such as open access publishing and digital scholarship are often difficult to consider since they offer new opportunities and problems. In this chapter, a number of positive and negative aspects are considered via metaphors.

- "Coronavirus and the Online Pivot": the shift to online learning presented issues for many educators and institutions, such as how to develop resilient models should a new out-break occur, and this chapter uses metaphors to explore some of the issues raised by the online pivot.

- "Online Pedagogy": the dominance of the lecture as the model for higher education has highlighted the paucity of other models, so in this chapter metaphors related to teaching methods are explored.

- "Conclusion: Using Metaphor Appropriately": this chapter examines some of the dangers of metaphor and draws together some of the themes that have arisen throughout the book.

CHAPTER 1

An Example of
Metaphorical Thinking

Before we go further with ed tech as the focus for metaphors, it is worth expanding on the role of metaphors in shaping how we approach a subject. In this book, we will examine the type of generative, or interactive, metaphor mentioned previously, which potentially allows us to think about a topic in a new manner and examine the use of existing metaphors in ed tech and how they have influenced the conversation on implementation. However, with both of these uses of metaphor, our existing views on ed tech will also influence how we then think about the validity of the metaphor itself. The mapping outlined in the introduction is not just one way from the base domain to the target domain, but there is a reverse influence from our knowledge of the target domain that shapes how we view the base domain. For example, if I propose a metaphor of LMS (learning management system or VLE [virtual learning environment]) as a "toolbox," and if you have used an LMS and have existing views on its usefulness, then they will determine to an extent how relevant the analogy is for you. It is perhaps beneficial to start the consideration of metaphors with an education example, but one that lacks the technology aspect, in which the function of the metaphors themselves can be highlighted without any contamination of existing views.

I have chosen to use some visual work realized for the open program at the UK Open University (UKOU) for this purpose, for three reasons. First, it is still within the domain of education and hopefully easily understood; second, it is likely to meet the criterion of being relatively unfamiliar to most readers, so I can focus on the role of metaphors themselves; third, the images provide a useful basis for starting the discussion on metaphors.

The open program at the UKOU is a multidisciplinary degree. When the UKOU was founded in 1969, the only option available was a BA(Open); there were no named degrees. This was an explicit attempt by the UKOU's founders to make a UKOU degree different not just in mode of study but also in substance. Students constructed their own degree profiles, meaning that the modules were truly modular and could be combined as students saw fit, with no predetermined set of modules. The UKOU's first vice-chancellor, Walter Perry (1976, p. 61), stated that "a student is the best judge of what [s]he wishes to learn and that [s]he should be given the maximum freedom of choice consistent with a coherent overall pattern." Cooke et al. (2018, p. 128) set out the benefits of the open degree approach:

> Open degrees provide a valued alternative to subject-specific degrees by offering students the opportunity to study a flexible, personalized degree, where they can choose the modules they wish to study, constrained only by the need to study a required number of credits at each level or stage of study. This approach provides students with access to a wide variety of subjects that match and build on their existing skills and knowledge to develop a personalized curriculum that reinforces their existing experience to meet their vocational needs and personal interests.

However, the concept of an open degree and its potential benefits for some learners can be difficult to convey in the current educational context, in which most students and educators think of degrees in terms of named degrees with prescribed pathways. To attempt to articulate some of the ideas about the open degree, the open program team worked with artist Bryan Mathers (who also created the artwork for this book) to develop a number of visual prompts. The outcomes of these sessions constitute the metaphors that we will examine in this chapter.

THE **OPEN** DEGREE

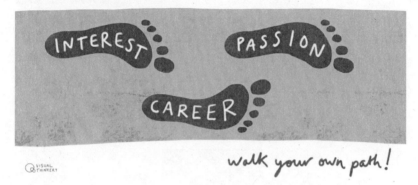

walk your own path!

"An uncharted pathway": the image shows footprints, like those left in sand, with the instruction to "walk your own path!" The intention was to highlight the unconstrained nature of the open degree in not following a predetermined path. By adding text to each footstep, the indication is that an open degree can be used to combine different aspects that motivate and make an individual, such as interest, career, and passion. The implication is that a conventional degree is both more constrained and might serve only one or two of these demands. A limitation of this metaphor is that the factors that contribute to the pathway might be more than the three indicated here and that there is no connection among the individual footprints.

"Brave learners": in this image, the shield bears the UKOU crest, and the legend declares that the open program is perfect for brave learners. The metaphor here is that the degree itself acts as a shield and facilitates the courage of learners in choosing to develop their own paths. A negative implication might be that learning itself is a dangerous enterprise through which the student has to battle.

"Pick and mix": this image uses the metaphor of a sweet shop offering a pick and mix selection, which allows consumers to place the sweets of their choice into one container. This metaphor conveys the personalized choice aspect of the degree and placing different elements into a single-size container (the sweet bag is analogous to the degree structure), but it is worth noting that some members of the program thought that it conveyed a negative message of indiscriminate combination rather than more purposeful construction. Pick and mix might also be culturally dependent and not resonate with some people.

"Space cadet": the UKOU celebrated its 50th anniversary in 2019, so the metaphor of the astronaut hearkened back to the moon landing, also in its golden jubilee year. But there is a further connotation of the theme of exploring and stepping where others have not. Many open program students take combinations of modules that no other student has taken. A negative aspect of this metaphor is that it might have connotations of a lonely learner in which there is no sense of a community or cohort.

CHOOSE THE PATH
OF GREATEST INTEREST

"Decision tree": this builds upon the metaphor of choosing and navigating one's own path. The text states "choose the path of greatest interest," suggesting that at any stage interest rather than a predetermined decision can dictate the path. As mentioned above, students choose from among a wide range of pathways, so at each of the nodes in the tree there are different numbers of student "leaves." This highlights that some pathway choices are more popular but that all are valid. There is also a temporal element to the metaphor in that the student is at the start of the journey, and the choices made can change as progress is made, and all options remain open. A limitation of this metaphor is that it might suggest that once a path is chosen there is no going back—for instance, that a choice down a science branch means that only science can be pursued, whereas that is not the case.

These are fairly simple metaphors, chosen for their visual impacts, but each of them carries subtle connotations that might or might not be apparent to the audience. There are also limitations to or possible negative inferences for each of them, which highlights that metaphors should be used with caution. The metaphors in these images also do not address some aspects of the open degree, and multidisciplinary study in general, such as the need for much knowledge to solve complex problems or the complementary relationship between such degrees and more specialist knowledge in teams.

These images also highlight how discussion on different metaphors is useful to teams. By talking in terms of metaphors, such as the pick and mix one, interesting points about priorities in the open degree can be raised. Using metaphors as a focus for dialogue and reflection to surface views is a productive approach, and the metaphors proposed in this book can be used for those purposes in HEIs.

The metaphors above were all developed to promote positive aspects of the program, but in this book, I take a nuanced position on ed tech. I use metaphors to apply a critical perspective to how ed tech is developed and implemented, I analyze other metaphors used by the sector to reveal how they frame discussions, and in some chapters I focus on how metaphors can help us to think about better implementation of ed tech for the benefit of learners. Like ed tech itself, metaphors are not intrinsically a beneficial way of approaching a subject, but in the selection that follows I hope that some are of use in your context and more generally that they encourage you to think creatively about the technology and its role in education, through metaphors of your own. As with the examples in this chapter, for each of the metaphors that follows, one could list negative or problematic issues with it. I have done this on occasion, but not systematically, since it might become repetitive, and it is unlikely that I could capture all possible alternative interpretations. However, I invite you to ask, "yes, but what about . . . ?" at the end of each chapter. Metaphors are never complete, always potentially hazardous and open to reinterpretation. It is this very process of thinking through them in relation to the topic of interest—ed tech in our case—that makes them useful.

CHAPTER 2

Thinking about Ed Tech

Educational technology is still a relatively new field in terms of digital technology, although it has a much longer tradition in terms of analogue artifacts, which can encompass papyrus, books, models, and engines. In *25 Years of Ed Tech* (Weller, 2020), I set out some of this recent history after the arrival of the web in mainstream society. This survey of developments from bulletin board systems to blockchain revealed that often it is not the technology itself that is significant but the surrounding social, economic, and bureaucratic structures. For instance, eportfolios allow learners to gather smaller pieces of digital outputs together into a portable portfolio. In many ways, this is a more desirable approach to assessment than the traditional high-stakes exam, allowing individuals to showcase their learning to different audiences and employers to assess the actual pieces of evidence against job criteria. They have had some success, but the COVID-19 pandemic has revealed how many institutions still rely on the final sat exam to assess understanding. The problem for more widespread eportfolio adoption is largely not a technical one; rather, it is based upon acceptance of this mode of assessment by learners, educators, employers, and society more widely. There is a good deal of entrenched practice among all of these groups that makes wholesale change difficult.

This example illustrates that ed tech often lacks a framework in which it can be understood, and any focus on only the technology misses the larger considerations and contexts within which it exists. In the first section of this chapter, I examine three prominent metaphors that arose and were commonly used when the internet was still relatively new and views of its potential were rooted in optimism but that now reveal some of the more complex and nefarious aspects of technology. This discussion sets the stage for a consideration of the longer-term social context of technology in general.

In the next section, I examine the appeal of ed tech to venture capitalists using a historical analogy to the appeal of castle building for Victorians. How the business of ed tech shapes much of our discussion on it is a theme of this book, and the aim of this metaphor is to consider the motivations, beyond purely financial ones, that drive much of this commercial interest.

In the subsequent section, I offer a contrast by proposing the metaphor of "rewilding," in which control over the environment is removed to allow a more diverse ecosystem to develop.

In the last section, I am interested in the dialogue of change (and resistance to change) that pervades much of the ed tech field. Higher education is often portrayed as being resistant to, or incapable of, change. It has not changed for 100 years is the common claim, but by comparing it to the book industry the changes and similarities over the past century can be demonstrated.

The Problem with the Internet Trinity

Some of the early metaphors of the internet illustrate how the initial optimism about positive social change has turned to a more dystopian perspective. Because the internet, and particularly the web and social media, are so pervasive now and form such an integral part of our everyday lives, there is a tendency to overlook how recent all of this change has been and how rapid the associated social adjustments have been. If the founding of the pre-web can be seen as the gestation of the internet's role in society, then since the 1990s we have been going through its childhood. This has been a time filled with optimism, charm, naïveté, and rapid development. We are now in the teenage years, which can be dark and moody but also positive, engaging, and realistic. It is a stage in which we and the technology seek meaning and our roles in the world.

One way to demonstrate this shift is to think of some of those early beliefs and sayings about the internet. They were couched in metaphors, and when we re-examine them now there are often aspects that are apparent that were not appreciated or intended when they were first proposed.

For example, it was commonly said in one form or another that "we're all broadcasters now" (e.g., Shirky, 2008), by which people meant that publishing content was no longer the privilege of those who worked in the media or owned a newspaper. This removal of the filter to publish remains the most powerful aspect of the internet. But thinking about the metaphor of broadcasters now, what we did not appreciate then was that it should also have meant "we all have the responsibility of broadcasters now." In a world where misinformation and fake news are disorientating to any notion of truth, to the extent that *post-truth* was the word of the year in 2016 (BBC News, 2016), how each one of us contributes to this problem becomes significant. Like broadcasters are supposed to, we have a responsibility to check the veracity of stories that we share, retweet, and amplify. Sadly, many broadcasters have also abandoned that principle. But the point remains: the liberation that we initially perceived masked the responsibility that came with it.

Caulfield (2019) proposes four moves toward building habits that protect against this kind of misinformation and therefore its redistribution. The four moves have the acronym SIFT.

- **S**top: ask whether the website or source of information is known and what the reputations of both the claim and the website are.

- **I**nvestigate the source: take 60 seconds to consider where it is from before reading it; doing so will help you to determine if it is worth your attention and, if it is, provide a better understanding of its significance and trustworthiness.

- **F**ind trusted coverage: sometimes it is not the particular article that is of interest but the *claim* that the article is making. You want to know if it is true or false. In these cases, it is useful to "find other coverage" that better suits your needs—more trusted, more in-depth, or maybe just more varied.

• Trace claims, quotations, and posts back to the original contexts: much of what we find on the internet has been stripped of context. In these cases, it is useful to go back to the original sources so that their contexts can be ascertained and thus whether the version shared was accurately presented.

SIFT is an example of the journalistic habits that we need to develop for ourselves in a world where everyone is a broadcaster.

James Boyle (1997) proposed an "internet trinity" or three fundamental beliefs that people held about the internet, at least in its early days. They can be seen as laws focused on the internet's seeming immunity from state regulation. Boyle argued that "this tripartite immunity came to be a kind of Internet Holy Trinity, [and] faith in it was a condition of acceptance into the community." If we examine each in turn, then a similar reinterpretation of the broadcaster's cliché in the current context can be revealed.

The first law of the internet trinity is that "the Net interprets censorship as damage and routes around it." This is a quotation attributed to John Gilmore (Boyle, 1997). This was and remains a powerful metaphor. It attributes agency to the internet; however, as long as one remains wary of attributing intention to a technology, it does seem to capture the internet's (or the community of internet users') ability to avoid forms of censorship and find alternatives. This is a result of how the internet itself is structured. As Boyle puts it, the internet's "distributed architecture and its technique of packet switching were built around the problem of getting messages delivered despite blockages, holes and malfunctions. Imagine the poor censor faced with such a system. There is no central exchange to seize and hold; messages actively 'seek out' alternative routes so that even if one path is blocked another may open up."

A plus for overcoming state censorship, then, but the flip side of this metaphor could be that "trolls will route around censorship."

Caulfield (2017) refers to the controversy of Gamergate, when women in the gaming industry suffered coordinated harassment as a "dry run for the apocalypse." He suggests that such activities, which might seem to be confined to a small community, are part of a broader movement in which "the rise of coordinated mal-information and harassment for political ends has much of its roots in the harassment of women online and misogyny in general." Similarly, Lees (2016) identifies Gamergate as a warning about the radicalization of the alt-right: "This hashtag was the canary in the coalmine, and we ignored it." Many of the systematic trolling and organized harassment techniques developed through the Gamergate community then spread further to the alt-right. Effectively, techniques were finessed there, and participants learned how to route around censorship in order to make previously extremist views part of the mainstream.

The second law of the internet trinity is that, "in Cyberspace, the First Amendment is a local ordinance," attributed to John Perry Barlow. This took the metaphor of the First Amendment of the US Constitution, whereby the government cannot pass laws restricting practice of religion, freedom of speech, and right to assembly and suggested that these were fundamental freedoms regardless of physical location. Boyle states that, "to the technological obstacles the Net raises against externally imposed content filtration, one must add the geographic obstacles raised by its global extent; since a document can as easily be retrieved from a server 5,000 miles away as one five miles away, geographical proximity and content availability are independent of each other." This meant that the significance of physical location and the ability to control someone's access to resources based upon that location are diminished. This failure to create a constitution of the internet, the romantic wild west notion, where anything goes, has fuelled the sense that free speech means freedom from consequences. It has also meant that we have state regulation of the internet in many places, increasing data surveillance, and the lack of a real regulatory (compared with a technical) framework to defend it. The First Amendment needed to be a global ordinance, but so did the accompanying restrictions on what is permissible.

The third and perhaps most fundamental law of the internet trinity that Boyle proposes is Stewart Brand's phrase "Information Wants to be

Free." Again, this is metaphorical in nature, applying intent to information. Such anthropomorphic thinking is problematic, but as with the first law it does provide a useful way of thinking about how the removal of the filter, the anonymous nature of the internet, and the immediate global distribution meant that it was difficult, if not impossible, to contain information. The famous Streisand effect (Masnick, 2005), whereby a clumsy attempt to censor or control information has the opposite effect of publicizing it more widely, particularly through social media, is an instance of this. Named after Barbra Streisand's attempt to remove pictures of her Malibu residence, it had the effect of greatly increasing views of it. Similar effects have been seen by companies or individuals that attempt to suppress information. More significantly, the notion that information wants to be free can be seen in the release of confidential documents, such as the extent of government surveillance revealed by Edward Snowden or Aaron Swartz's release of JSTOR academic articles.

So, in many respects, information seemingly does want to be free. But maybe misinformation wants to be free *more*. And that poses real problems for a society. Aggressive recommendation algorithms in platforms such as YouTube and Pinterest mean that extremist views, conspiracy theories, and misinformation spread quickly. In addition, social media function by promoting views that provoke strong reactions, operating an "outrage economy" (Harvey, 2018), with bloggers, columnists, and media outlets all seeking traffic through clickbait articles. In this environment, factual information often struggles to compete against a system that favours misinformation. As a result, political entities have become adept at manipulating this tendency of information. For example, the site Wikileaks might be seen as an embodiment of the principle, but it has also been accused of being a vehicle for conspiracy theories and supporting an anti–Hillary Clinton stance during the American election in 2016. The initial metaphor of information wanting to be free was largely seen in a positive light, but when this tendency became manipulated and weaponized the very lack of control that made it appealing meant that the damage was difficult to limit.

To return to the initial point, from a long-view perspective, it is not surprising that we're now going through these struggles with our relationship with the internet. It is all still relatively new, and society

really has not had anything like this before. This makes it more important that we seek to address the issues now and reflect on where the
internet is heading rather than see it as neutral or something beyond
our control. Analyzing what these initial metaphors promised and how
they have altered over the past 20 or so years provides a means to reflect
on our changing relationship with the internet. This relationship is at
the core of how we view, develop, and implement ed tech.

The Lure of Ed Tech

In this section, I want to explore why venture capitalists and technology start-ups are seemingly so obsessed with developing solutions for
education. We will look at the "education is broken" metaphor later, but
it seems that barely a week goes past without some new solution being
announced that will "fix" some part of education. The obvious answer
to the question of why ed tech is attractive is that it is seen as a lucrative
investment—the global market for education was estimated at $6 tril-
lion in 2019 (Nead, 2019), and the global shift to online education in 2020
has increased the appeal of this market. There is also the perception
that the education sector is slow and ripe for change, which appeals to
both investors and developers. These are undoubtedly significant factors,
but I suspect that there is something else in the psychological mix that
makes it so appealing, which can be thought of as a desire for a form of
legitimacy and permanence. To illustrate this, I will use the metaphor
of the industrial revolution and how architectural symbols of permanence appealed to the newly rich barons, in particular the construction
of a fairy-tale castle in Wales.

Castell Coch: A Brief History

Castell Coch (Welsh for "Red Castle") is situated above the village of
Tongwynlais, on the outskirts of Cardiff in the United Kingdom. The
ruins of an 11th-century castle and the surrounding land were acquired
in 1760 by John Stuart, Third Earl of Bute. His great-grandson, John
Crichton-Stuart, the Third Marquis of Bute, inherited the castle in 1848
(Davies, 1981). The landed estates, and particularly ownership of the Cardiff docks, which had become the busiest coal-exporting docks in the

world, made him one of the wealthiest men in the world. A keen medievalist, Crichton-Stuart employed the prominent architect of the High Victorian style, William Burges, to reconstruct the castle as a summer hunting retreat (McLees, 2005).

In collaboration with the Marquis, Burges developed a design in the style of medieval, fairy-tale castles. The exterior was constructed from 1875 to 1879, but Burges died in 1881 after contracting a chill on a visit to the castle, and its interior was completed by 1891 according to his plans. Despite its intended aim as a hunting lodge, the castle was not used often, and it is largely viewed as part of the Victorian fashion for follies (Andrews, 2001).

The position of the castle overlooks the main valley route into Cardiff and renders it visible from the city. This made it a constant reminder to the populace of Bute's wealth and influence in the newly emerging industrial centre, as did the central Cardiff Castle. The site is significant when the context of Cardiff is considered at the time of construction of the castle. This period can be considered as a belated example of what Peter Borsay (1989) termed the "urban renaissance." Borsay argues that after 1700 many English towns underwent a renaissance characterized by uniform design, street planning, a growing middle-class population, and increased leisure facilities such as assembly halls, public gardens, and theatres. A number of conditions then arose to see a shift from towns focused less on their rural positions than on their services. Borsay provides the role of leisure as an example of such a shift in identity and function. The urban renaissance was largely unseen in Wales, however, which lacked major industry prior to the nineteenth century. Towns such as Brecon acted as agricultural market towns, but the geography made transportation difficult between many Welsh settlements, which limited their trade.

However, many of the features that Borsay (1989) sets out as being characteristic of an 18th-century urban renaissance can be seen in 19th-century Cardiff, accompanied by population growth. Allied with this population growth were many of the public amenities that Borsay cites as characteristic of an urban renaissance, for instance a gas act in 1837 for public lighting, a waterworks act in 1850, and signs of leisure such as a racecourse in 1855. This is in contrast to the experience of the poor in Cardiff, which after the Poor Law of 1834 developed a workhouse in 1836. This soon proved to be inadequate for the expanding population, and a new workhouse was constructed in 1881 (Higginbotham, 2012).

Castell Coch as a Representation of Power

This overview provides the context within which Castell Coch was constructed and how it could be interpreted by the local population. The urban renaissance and industrial revolution meant that this was a time of great social upheaval—the trade union movement was a significant force in South Wales, and the Rebecca Riots of 1839–1844 in Wales (which we will look at in a later metaphor) had demonstrated that social unrest could flare up violently (Williams, 1955). The political activism of the Chartists in the South Wales coal fields similarly highlighted that the feudal order was in decline (Williams, 1959). These social upheavals caused great anxiety among the elite, with the railway merchants proclaiming that "the late Chartist and Rebecca riots sufficiently evince that Wales will become in as bad a state as Ireland, unless the means of improvement are given to it" (Railway Intelligence, 1846).

From this perspective, then, Castell Coch can be viewed not simply as an indulgence of an interest in medievalism but also as a deliberate attempt to lay claim to the historical immutability of the position of the aristocracy. This view is further reinforced by the siting of Castell Coch on an existing ruin. The original site dates back to the Normans and was rebuilt in 1277 to control the Welsh. As Wales faced another potential rebellion in the industrial age, the reconstruction of Castell Coch can be interpreted as a signal to the longevity of power. The decision by Burges to incorporate elements of the earlier castle, particularly noticeable in the cellar, reinforces this connection with past representations of power.

Although the family of the Third Marquis of Bute could point to several generations of wealth, they were not part of the landed gentry dating back to Napoleonic times. In South Wales, Philip Jenkins (1984) argues, there was a shift in the gentry from ancient landed families to a new landed elite after approximately 1760. These new families sought to establish an "ancient gentry": "For the new ruling class, newness was politically damaging, while antiquity could be a considerable asset. If they could only assert their historical roots they could claim to be part of a natural and immemorial rural order" (p. 46). In this context, the faux romantic style of the castle can be interpreted as an extension of power. By evoking romantic notions of medieval ages, and building upon the site of a Norman castle, the message of Castell Coch is one of the permanence of power. The immutability of the aristocracy is presented as both reassuring and unquestionable. Williamson (2007) highlights this conscious manipulation of "symbols of the past" in order to hide a very modern use of land ownership rights and thus avoid possible confrontation. For example, West (2012, p. 141) demonstrates how landscape gardens were "spaces deliberately removed from production" and then presented as aesthetic objects. Castell Coch can be viewed similarly as an artistic creation removed from the original function, in this case military defence, of the original.

The Victorian period was one of immense social change, as has been highlighted by some of the examples in Cardiff given above. This generated wealth for many new families but also much nostalgia. Although the wealthy benefited from the change, they also sought to control it and root it back in times that they envisaged as more stable. Describing Lady Bute's bedroom in Castell Coch, Crook (1981, p. 283) calls it "a retreat for some lovelorn Tennysonian maiden." The castle can be seen as one of the last large-scale constructions in the Victorian gothic revival style developed by architects Augustus Pugin and George Gilbert Scott. Writing of Pugin, Hill (2008, p. 3) says that he saw the "Middle Ages as a model not just for architecture but for society." This reflects not just the aesthetic appeal of medievalism for Burges and the Marquis of Bute but also the social appeal of being associated with an unquestionable hierarchical, feudal system.

The Ed Tech Equivalent

If we view the digital revolution as a social force similar to the industrial revolution, then it creates similar challenges to established power. Many of the newly super-wealthy of the digital revolution have invested in education. Mark Zuckerberg of Facebook has issued over $100 million in grants to education through the Chan Zuckerberg Initiative (Barnum, 2019). Facebook is attempting to position its platform as an educational tool, with Facebook Education aiming to create "the programs, tools, and products to build diverse learning communities that bring the world closer together" (Facebook, 2021). Similarly, Bill Gates of Microsoft has established the Bill and Melinda Gates Foundation, which has a Global Education Program with the goal of "provid[ing] education systems around the world with better information, evidence, tools and approaches that can help improve primary and secondary education, with an emphasis on foundational learning in primary grades" (Gates Foundation, 2021). Microsoft also positions itself as a global provider of educational software with the goal of "empowering every student on the planet to achieve more" (Microsoft, 2021). Amazon founder Jeff Bezos announced in 2018 that he intended to create a network of non-profit schools where "the child will be the customer" (Kastrenakes, 2018).

Although there is a mixture of sensible business acumen in these actions and probably a genuine desire to help with education, there is also a desire by the newly super-rich to position themselves, and more fundamentally the Silicon Valley approach, in a dominant position in the digital landscape, just as Castell Coch was in the physical one. Williamson (2017, p. 265) proposes five Silicon Valley "innovations" that ed tech companies seek to develop, including start-up schools and "student-centred high tech homeschooling approaches," arguing that they demonstrate how "Silicon Valley is seeking to reproduce its centrality to the techno-economic revolution" in the educational space. With the ed tech investment market forecast to grow to $342 billion by 2025 (HolonIQ, 2020), this central positioning is not an exercise in altruism.

But beyond financial gains, also evident here is a desire by the newly powerful and wealthy to ally themselves with symbols of longevity. In the physical world, these were castles and manor houses. In the digital world, it is education and governance. Education is often decried for being slow to change, for being stuck in the past, but whether tech companies realize it or not these are exactly the values that they seek to appropriate. Education is a (generally) recognized universal good. It has longevity, history, and social capital. These characteristics, as much as the millions of users with associated dollars, are assets that tech companies seek to acquire. As with Castell Coch, this association with symbols of permanence strengthens the position of the powerful.

The message of Castell Coch was that it was physically unassailable, and by implication so was the position of those who owned it. This gave legitimacy to their new-found wealth, and with legitimacy comes an acceptance and a decline in criticism. Just as the association with medievalism emphasized a "natural" hierarchy for the Marquis of Bute, so too education proposes a social good perspective for technology. People are less inclined to question algorithms, ethics, or market control when the companies can claim to be educating 20 million people in developing nations with their platforms.

This does not mean that higher education should eschew technology and technology companies—far from it, for we have a duty to ensure that learners get the most from technology and to use it to teach in new ways and reach new audiences. We should also recognize that universities often operate as commercial entities themselves and have their own drivers. But education should not sell itself too cheaply in potential partnerships. The conversation is often positioned as one of either education as consumers or technology companies as saviours. However, it is important to appreciate that tech companies gain something else from association with education, and that should not be given away lightly, in terms of either finance or principle.

Rewilding Ed Tech

Rewilding is the restoration of an ecosystem to a less managed one, where plants and animals that cannot flourish in intensively farmed or cultivated land can once again grow sustainable populations. Monbiot (2013) states that even nature reserves are extremely overmanaged: "The ecological disasters we call nature reserves are often kept in this depleted state through intense intervention: cutting and burning any trees that return; grazing by domestic animals at greater densities and for longer periods than would ever be found in nature." He goes on to argue that the solution to this depleted state is rewilding, which involves "reintroducing missing animals and plants, taking down the fences, blocking the drainage ditches, culling a few particularly invasive exotic species but otherwise standing back. It's about abandoning the Biblical doctrine of dominion which has governed our relationship with the natural world."

Tree (2018) recounts her experience of rewilding the Knepp estate in Sussex. She considers rewilding to be a process in which landowners have to let go to an extent and allow ecology to take its own course. There are different ways to approach rewilding. The most well-known is the reintroduction of large predators, such as wolves. The reintroduction of wolves from Canada into Yellowstone Park in 1995 has been deemed largely a success, both the wolves and the ecosystem as a whole flourishing. By controlling elk numbers, the height of willow saplings has increased, because fewer elk graze them. This is an example of what is termed "trophic cascade," in which the introduction or removal of an apex predator can cause changes throughout the ecosystem. Similarly, the number of grizzly bears has increased because of increased carcasses to feed on (Smith & Bangs, 2009). This top-down approach (in terms of the food chain) can be contrasted with a bottom-up approach in which rewilding commences at the bottom of the food chain with the reintroduction of small-scale flora and the removal of some invasive species, which then allows for the process of succession to establish a habitat that attracts and supports wildlife. This can be realized through seed dispersal or the planting of tree seedlings, as in Scotland by the Trees for Life project. Often rewilding projects, such as that at the Knepp estate, combine both approaches, introducing new plants as well as larger species such as hogs and deer.

Before turning to the application of rewilding to ed tech, it is worth emphasizing that metaphors drawn from nature are probably the most prevalent but the most dangerous. Making appeals to what is deemed "natural" and applying them to any form of human endeavour have led to justifications for social Darwinism, misogyny, and repression, with the implication that certain states are naturally occurring and therefore inevitable. We should approach any metaphor that draws on nature with caution. The intention in this case is to investigate whether the two approaches to rewilding hold any value in considering the range of technology used in higher education. The collection of different technologies is often referred to as constituting an ecosystem, of course a metaphor that comes laden with many assumptions but also offers some useful reminders about how technologies interact with each other, can change over time, and fulfil specific functions (or environmental niches).

Much of the early enthusiasm for ed tech stemmed from the facts that it was fast, cheap, and out of control (Groom & Lamb, 2014). However, as elearning gained significance and occupied a more central role in the university system, the associated technology became more robust and controllable. This was inevitable and beneficial in many ways—students don't want the system that they need to submit an assignment at midnight to be flaky or to spend their study time overcoming barriers in using a technology. But, as a result, there has been a loss of some of the innovation that was prevalent when there were greater freedoms as university processes and regulations have solidified around enterprise systems, such as the VLE or LMS. The deployment of such systems necessitates the development of administrative structures and processes that are then framed in terms of the specific technology. Thus, institutions have roadmaps, guidelines, training programs, and reporting structures, all of which help to embed the chosen tool. This in effect creates a tool-focused solution—if educators want to achieve something in their courses, and they ask their IT, or educational support, team for help, often the answer will be couched in terms of "what is the moodle (or institutional tool) way of implementing this?" or "that isn't in our LMS road plan." We will look at VLE/LMS metaphors in more detail in a later chapter, but in terms of the analogy here this establishes the kind of aggressive monoculture that intensive farming or land management has produced in many countries. As with the LMS, there are undoubtedly benefits to intensive farming, and it has increased productivity, allowing for affordable foods and robust supply chains. But it comes with an environmental cost (there are other costs too in terms of subsidies, globalization, and so on, but they are outside the scope of this discussion). Farmers grow a limited number of crops, and the use of fertilizers often means that the soil is not suitable for other plants. Both by intention and then through habitat formation, variety is reduced.

Having established the productive habitat of the LMS, though, many now seek more variety in the ed tech ecosystem. They might want to introduce tools into the ecosystem that would encourage some of the innovation that we saw previously. However, as with introducing apex predators, it has to be done carefully; just as Yellowstone National Park officials did not want tourists attacked by wolves, so too ed tech teams don't want students caught in frustrations with unusable systems. The two approaches to rewilding offer pointers here. A bottom-up approach might be to introduce some small-scale, low-impact tools, such as SPLOT (2021), or smallest/simplest, possible/portable, learning/living, open/online, tool/technology, and the argument is that publishing in the open web is powerful, but too many open web tools (e.g., blogs) are seen as technical and specialist, thus creating a barrier for many to participate in this open web. The aim is to create simple tools, for instance a form, that reduce the barrier to such publication. The team behind SPLOT (notably Alan Levine and Brian Lamb) state two key principles: "Make it as easy as possible to post activity to the open web in an appealing and accessible way [and] allow users to do so without creating accounts or providing any required personal information."

Such tools can encourage some of the pedagogical innovation required without becoming an institution-wide tool. Groom (2017) suggests that often educators and students "don't want to be faced with a 'Hello World!' post. In fact, they don't even want to hear the word 'WordPress.' They just want a tool that helps them accomplish a fairly simple task that, in turn, helps them create a focused community-driven, engaging assignment."

The more top-down approach could be to introduce a number of enterprise systems, or ones that can allow for adaptation, but an alternative would be to tackle the policy issues such as incentivizing the use of such tools, developing an IT infrastructure capable of supporting them, allocating resources for development, and removing different barriers. In this model, it is also necessary to create a cultural context in which students themselves see the value in such experimentation and are not penalized for it.

Rewilding offers another element to the metaphor in terms of ecotones. These are the areas of transition between two different biological communities, for example reed beds between river and forest. They might be seen as analogous to the transition between higher education and employment or society. Rewilding might have a role to play here, for example making the HEI technological ecosystem more like that of the wider internet. However, as Bump (2018) highlights, rewilding can also have a negative impact, with moose playing an important role in transporting nutrients across ecotones, and this can be affected by trophic rewilding with the introduction of wolves. Similarly, ed tech rewilding can negatively affect students' performance or the robustness of such systems and thus limit the transition of skills and related evidence to the workplace. As mentioned previously, though rewilding is often beneficial for biological diversity, it is not the most effective or efficient means of food production to feed large populations. In a similar vein, a looser, more flexible ed tech system might not be efficient in terms of students' use of time or in achieving grades.

These examples might be stretching the rewilding metaphor beyond a useful framing, but they demonstrate the type of further extension and possible negative connotations of any given metaphor raised in the chapter on metaphorical thinking. For my purposes, rewilding offers one means to think about the ed tech culture that we have developed in higher education and whether it is sufficiently diverse to meet the needs of students and educators. Davis (2015) has also proposed rewilding as a metaphor for education: "What if we removed the fences, where instead of focusing on managing experiences for students from the top on down, we co-create experiences with students from the bottom up?" As with rewilding, the aim is to allow a more sustainable, varied system to develop, which perhaps better reflects the broader environment outside a university.

Book Reading and Change in Higher Education

Among the articles that offer new models for education, there is often a claim that education has remained unchanged for hundreds of years. Many of these articles focus on schools as the largest sector of education, but their argument is often applied to higher education also. For example, Parr (2012) combines the broken and unchanged argument in an article entitled "We Know Our Education System Is Broken, So Why Can't We Fix It?" As he asks, "how many industries that were around 100 years ago—and are still around today—are making their products almost the exact same way? . . . How about the American classroom? Our method of teaching hasn't radically changed over the past century. It's stuck, it's dated, and it's in need of radical transformation."

The basic argument in such pieces is that we have an education system that was designed for an industrial age, that we are now in a post-industrial age, and ergo that the system is faulty. Watters (2015) examines in detail the flawed history in such accounts, arguing that "phrases like 'the industrial model of education,' 'the factory model of education,' and 'the Prussian model of education' are used as a 'rhetorical foil' in order to make a particular political point—not so much to explain the history of education, as to try to shape its future." She also highlights that this argument dates back as far as 1932, with the urge to create a narrative that demands an upgrade. Here the "factory model of schooling" acts as a metaphor shaping our thinking about education in order to make a particular solution seem inevitable.

However, such accounts deliberately do not mention that a good deal of change has happened in the education sector, at primary, secondary, and tertiary levels, that often is not immediately apparent. If you were to go to a university campus, then *superficially* it looks as though things are largely unchanged from 100 years ago. The sports centre is better, the cafeteria serves different food, but there are still lectures, laboratories, and students sitting around on the grass. But these similarities mask real technological and demographic changes that have taken place, particularly over the past 20 years.

First, the concept of the traditional student—someone who leaves home at 18 and studies full time at a university—is no longer dominant. Many students live at home, study part time, study at a distance, or belong to the "mature" group (i.e., over the age of 22) (Cruse et al., 2018).

Second, the role of technology has become much more central. Imagine turning off teaching and learning systems at a university. Many universities would simply be unable to function. Students submit assignments, access teaching material, use digital library resources, use software for research, engage in group work, and socialize via these systems. Although I have many reservations about the LMS path, this technology is central in most universities. Even relatively uninteresting technologies (from a pedagogical perspective) such as lecture capture can have profound impacts for many students. The online pivot demonstrated that the university could function without the campus but not without the technology.

These differences are in addition to changes to the support structures in place and the experiences of many students. In short, a university experience now would be very different from that of 50 or 100 years ago, although aspects of it would be recognizable.

I want to explore further the claim that "education hasn't changed in a century," looking at the elements of that statement that are true (and why that is not necessarily a bad thing) and those that are false, by way of an analogy. Imagine that it is commonly stated as fact that "reading hasn't changed since the time of Dickens." To take the true aspect first, we could take a photo of someone reading a book printed on paper (maybe even a Dickens novel) while sitting in a chair in front of a fire. If you could go back in time, then you could show this image to Dickens, and he would declare that indeed reading has not changed. The first question to ask, then, is why would you want reading to change? Why is the *absence* of change deemed a bad thing? Reading a book is a good way to convey an idea or a story and an enjoyable and enriching thing to do. That this has not changed significantly in 150 years is a testament to its value, not a sign of its weakness.

Next, we can look at why this statement, though true in some respects, is also false. There are undoubtedly core similarities between reading now and reading in the time of Dickens, but there are also significant differences not revealed by that superficial analysis of the photo of an archetypal reader. For example, there have been significant changes in the following areas.

- The format: sales from online retail channels in 2018 showed that 45.1% were print, 24.5% ebooks, and 13.7% audiobooks (Rowe, 2019).

- The book retail industry: online retailers such as Amazon account for the majority of sales, with online retail accounting for $8.03 billion and physical retail $6.90 billion in 2018 (Rowe, 2019).

- The publishing process: digitization has made self-publishing easy, and selling self-published books via Amazon, which offers up to 70% royalties to authors, means that they are now bypassing traditional publishers.

- The novel genre: for example, compare a William S. Burroughs book, graphic novel, or fan fiction with a novel by Dickens.

- The context: reading now competes for leisure attention with gaming, on-demand television, cinema, and the internet.

So, any statement that nothing has changed does not recognize that reading now is a very different experience from what it was in 1840, and the book industry itself has changed considerably.

If we now return to the industrial education argument, then we see a similar pattern. First, there are significant similarities, so the statement is true in some respects. If you look at education now and in the 1900s, then there are some things that you would recognize: we send students to a central place, we have a physical library, we group learners in schools by age and ability, we have teachers. As with reading, these aspects might be unchanging because they work well. Whenever people propose that they want to revolutionize (or entirely do away with) the school or university system, their lack of a viable alternative that works for *all* learners—regardless of motivation, ability, or parental engagement—is often apparent. To realize this, a robust system is required. So, the absence of change so deplored by many might indicate that viable alternatives are not available. The start-up AltSchool failed to create a new school system, despite considerable investment from the likes of Mark Zuckerberg, partly because the vision of personalized learning was very difficult to realize for all children (Greene, 2019).

Second, we need to consider what is wrong with the statement. As with the Dickens example, it actually ignores many significant changes.

- Use of technology: most schools and HEIs have their own LMS and use electronic whiteboards, computer suites, et cetera.

- Changes in curriculum: although there seems to be a cyclical call for "back to basics" in school education, the range of subjects available to children has expanded and adapted considerably. The tertiary-level curriculum is constantly in flux, responding to new developments and demands.

- Changes in pedagogy: groupwork and a greater focus on coursework have allowed for different modes of teaching.

- Increased professionalization of educators: the associated structures of lessons, roles, and legal and reporting mechanisms for educators mean that they are operating in a very different context compared with that of their historical counterparts.

- Access to resources: they are no longer limited to the physical resources in the school library.

- Increased access to education: although elitism and the differing quality of education remain issues both within any one country and globally, access to good-quality education is now much more of a reality for many children, with the number of out-of-school children declining from 377 million in 2000 to 263 million in 2016, although it has plateaued over the past few years (UNESCO, 2016). Access to higher education has increased significantly since the 1960s in many countries, with global higher education enrolment growing from 32 million in 1970 to 214 million in 2015 and predicted to reach 594 million by 2040 (Calderon, 2018).

When we take these developments into account, education in 2021 is quite different from that in 1921. This is not to suggest that there are not significant changes that could be made within the education system, and more work can be done to improve access to education for all. For example, the Finnish approach to schooling is often cited as having a better attitude to assessment, curriculum, grouping, mental health, and pedagogy (e.g., Weale, 2019), and deploying this approach more widely might have significant benefits.

How, then, can we reconcile these two elements of seeming resistance to change yet large-scale innovation within education? I suggest that both books and education have what might be termed a "core of immutability": that is, some essential aspect that does not alter. Indeed, this essence is part of the reason that we give them high social value, they echo back through history, and they evoke generally positive emotions. For both, this core relates to the individual focus on a task conducted largely in the mind—indulgence in what is essentially a cognitive art form. Both are also fundamentally human—maybe AI can write decent books in the future, and maybe it can provide a reasonable level of support, but it can never quite capture that human element that is part of their appeal.

Recognizing, cherishing, and protecting this core of immutability allow us to engage in technological experimentation with it without threatening to destroy it. The analogy of books and reading to education highlights how this core is something to be valued but can be susceptible to change.

CHAPTER 3

Ed Tech as an Undiscipline

Educational technology can seem like a strange field in which to work. For those of us in it, we are not even sure how to refer to it—a field, subject, topic, practice, discipline? In 2016, Eddie Maloney proposed that educational technology should be considered a discipline if it is to develop (Raths, 2016). Watters (2016) argued against this idea, proposing an alternative framing: "I want to suggest that what we need instead of a discipline called 'education technology' is an undisciplining. We need criticism at the center of our work."

What constitutes a discipline is complex and itself a matter of some debate. Krishnan (2009) suggests that disciplines have the following characteristics:

- a particular object of research;

- a body of accumulated specialist knowledge referring to the object of research;

- theories and concepts that can organize the accumulated specialist knowledge effectively;

- use-specific terminologies or a specific technical language adjusted to the research object;

- developed specific research methods according to the specific research requirements; and

- some institutional manifestation in the form of subjects taught at universities or colleges, respective academic depart- ments, and professional associations connected to it.

Kreber (2010) distinguishes between subjects as what is looked at and disciplines as what is looked through or with, emphasizing that the concepts and methods unify a discipline. There has been a long-running criticism of disciplines in that they constrain knowledge and create artificial boundaries. It is frequently proclaimed that interdisciplinary approaches are desirable, but disciplines seem to be stubbornly resistant to such approaches. In 1990, Klein bemoaned the lack of interdisciplin- ary progress: "Since the 1970s there has been an exponential growth of publications on interdisciplinarity. . . . Good scholarship on the subject does exist, but it is underused" (p. 14), and little has changed since then.

Given the problems of disciplines, it might seem to be counter- productive to want to create one when so many are seeking to break down the boundaries of existing ones. However, the potential desirabil- ity of having ed tech considered a discipline can be seen in some of the characteristics above, particularly in agreed terminologies. Other bene- fits would include a framework within which a range of perspectives could be incorporated. One criticism of ed tech is that people come to it from other disciplines and often are unaware of fundamental work in the field. A recognized ed tech discipline in fact might be interdisciplin- ary and incorporate components from psychology, sociology, education, computer science, statistics, et cetera. This would help to establish a canonical body of texts, presumably, with which most people in the field are familiar.

Another criticism of ed tech is that it lacks rigour. Claims are often based upon anecdotes, small trials, or just hopes about the power of tech- nology. As well as establishing common content, an ed tech disciple can establish good principles and processes in terms of evaluating evidence.

Finally, a discipline creates a body against which criticism can act. By way of analogy, let us consider art history, which used to be predominantly about the history of art. Starting with Vasari's *Lives of the Artists*, originally published in 1550, it focused on the "great" artists and their works. Later it shifted to talking about styles as a way of framing the history of art. But in the 1970s there was a reaction to these approaches, bringing in Marxist, feminist, and multicultural perspectives. The implicit assumptions in the previous approaches were directly challenged, leading to the new art history. Now art history is as much about "art history the discipline and practice" as it is about "the history of art." By making ed tech a discipline, there is the possibility that a similar perspective will be facilitated. We can have a new art history only if there was an old art history. When a subject becomes a discipline, it is not long before you get a version of it prefaced by the word *critical*.

I proposed some of the arguments above in a blog post (Weller, 2016). The post generated many comments that generally weighed against the idea of a formal discipline. These arguments came in three related forms. The first argument was that, as we have seen, disciplines are generally restraining, leading to silos that can be difficult to overcome. This is problematic for all subjects but particularly for ed tech, which pervades all other disciplines.

The second argument was that many of the powerful critical voices in ed tech currently come from women and people of colour. Any discipline has the effect of excluding, or at least privileging, some voices to create a canon and strict legitimacy of the methods, research programs, and views permitted. So, far from allowing a more critical perspective, it could lead to less alternative views.

The third argument was that it would constrain how ed tech operates and limit its role. In the comments on the blog post, McMillan Cotton suggested that how a discipline works is contrary to how much of ed tech operates, in a more networked manner: "Ed-tech as we currently practice and understand it could not do the necessary work of exclusion, rank ordering and symbolic exchange that institutions require of disciplines."

Similarly, Bowles (2019) commented that a disciplinary approach would be restrictive: "To me the school of thought we could call 'edtech' accommodates a community of purpose, enriched by coming from different disciplinary perspectives. But the industrial formation we could call 'disciplines' is a whole other mess of problems, not least of which is the folly of categorical thought."

On reflection, these criticisms carried the day in my view. Although ed tech is flawed in a number of respects, for example in its historical amnesia and its occasional uncritical approach, these flaws are not addressed by making ed tech conform to a strict disciplinary boundary. Ed tech is rich precisely because people enter it from different fields, bringing a range of perspectives to bear, and it is applied to different disciplines that have their own requirements and challenges.

It seemed, then, that a better way of framing ed tech was required than simply traditional academic disciplines. In this chapter, I want to consider three ways of thinking about ed tech as an "undiscipline" via three separate metaphors. The first is to think of ed tech as a suitcase in which people can pack vastly different components while retaining the overall purpose. The second is to consider notions of collective identity that those in the area of ed tech might share, like those who identify themselves as belonging to a particular nation. The role of artifacts in establishing these identities is significant, and we will explore the analogy of national museums. The third is to use the metaphor of mudlarking, whereby people along a river extract artifacts shaped by the river for preservation. This potentially captures the more dynamic nature of the ed tech field, in which the practitioner operates in an environment in constant flux.

These metaphors might seem to be solipsistic in thinking about ed tech in a manner interesting only to a small group of academics. But how those in the field view their own practice is important for shaping the stories about it, and in the absence of unifying views it is easy for an external narrative to be imposed on it.

The Ed Tech Suitcase

Consider packing a suitcase for a trip. It will contain many different items—clothes, toiletries, books, electrical items, maybe food and drink or gifts. Some of these items bear a relation to others, for example types of clothes, and others are seemingly unrelated, for example a hair dryer. Each brings its own function, which has a separate existence and relates to other items outside the case, but within the case they form a new category, that of "items I need for my trip." In this sense, the suitcase resembles the ed tech field, or at least a gathering of ed tech individuals, for example at a conference.

If you attend a chemistry conference and have lunch with strangers, then it is highly likely that nearly all of them will have chemistry doctorates. This is not the case at an ed tech conference, where the lunch table might have people with expertise in computer science, philosophy, psychology, art, history, or engineering. This diversity is a strength of the field, although it brings with it issues of the lack of a shared knowledge base, as set out above. The contents of the individual suitcases representing the chemistry conference will have many similarities, but the ed tech suitcases will contain many different items. From this perspective, then, the aim is not to make the items of the suitcases standard but to find means by which they meet the overall aim of usefulness for each individual and are not random items not needed. This suggests a different way of approaching ed tech beyond making it a discipline.

Techniques for developing commonality among individuals can include running primers for people new to ed tech, explicitly bringing multidisciplinary perspectives to bear on tech issues, having common problems to address, crowd-sourcing principles, and so on. This is akin to making the suitcase items individual while also making their combined contents mutually useful. The approach is to reach some form of consensus, but that consensus itself is fluid and changeable, varying over time and location, just as the contents of the suitcase will vary depending on specific trips. This perspective on ed tech allows it to remain more fluid and malleable than a discipline.

Another view of the suitcase metaphor is not as the container for the field but as the case for the individual ed tech practitioner, who will bring items for the case that are unique to them representing their background, and over time the case itself will become customized. Just as people add stickers to their cases recording their trips, so too the case becomes a record of the journey itself. There is a German metaphor for a case, a *Reisebegleiter*, which translates as "travelling companion" but also carries connotations of something that goes with you through life. This creates an interplay between temporary and longer-term travel.

Deepwell (2020) explores this interplay by referring to an artwork that she developed called the *Travelling Monument Kit*. This was a suitcase that contained representations of monuments, such as miniature Eiffel Tower models. The artwork explores "the relationship between travelling and permanence. Travelling is all about leaving things behind, discovering new ones and changing perspectives. . . . [I]t's about change. Monuments are normally fixed in place and time, permanent markers of things to be remembered." The *Travelling Monument Kit* is a suitcase that reverses this notion and contains permanent objects or monuments of travel. It "explores how we can create lasting meaning amidst change. . . . It's about creating something solid and strong, a connection, to bring things into perspective."

For the individual ed tech practitioner, the suitcase becomes something akin to the *Travelling Monument Kit* across their career. The "monuments" include original disciplinary knowledge, and as they progress to unknown areas in ed tech they seek to make these connections and gather more "monuments." They might be technologies, conceptual frameworks, methodologies, or connections with other individuals, events, or projects. This perspective emphasizes two aspects that ed tech should seek to preserve and cherish. The first is that it recognizes previous experience as valid in this context; the second is that it is unique and unpredictable. Everyone's kit will be different, and it is by developing that kit that the person brings understanding to an often new and changing area. Again, such a perspective might suggest ways of thinking about and facilitating this in ed tech. We can provide the equivalent of travel guides to help navigate these travels, without prescribing the actual journey, and portfolio accreditation such as the Association for Learning Technology's certified membership process, which operates on a portfolio allowing recognition of different experiences.

Art History and National Identity

The second analogy in considering ed tech as an undiscipline is to reflect on notions of collective identity, in this case how art relates to national identity, itself a nebulous concept like that of belonging to a discipline. Art history often has a complex relationship with notions of nationality, heritage, politics, and history. This relationship varies across nations, time periods, and forms of art, and in this section, I will focus on the Welsh context. Hewison (1987) was one of the first critics to question the generally accepted heritage approach that often focused on preserving country houses, stately homes, and national monuments. In *The Heritage Industry*, he argued that museums were guilty of creating a sanitized, detached version of the past, divorced from much of its reality, controversy, and connection to modern living, which stifled the capacity for creative change. Writing of English heritage, Hewison made the strong claim that, "individually, museums are fine institutions, dedicated to the high values of preservation, education and truth; collectively, their growth in numbers points to the imaginative death of this country" (p. 8). Wright (1985) similarly criticized what he termed the "museumification" of the heritage industry and its influence on modern consciousness, arguing that the national past addresses the question of "cultural authenticity," but this is distinct from a question of historiographical truth and is subject to specific, and highly political, interpretations.

Although Wright (1985) and Hewison (1987) were writing about the English heritage tradition, similar critiques have arisen elsewhere. There have been recent shifts in approaches to heritage, however. For example, Orange (2008) observes that there has been a more recent shift from the traditional focus of heritage to include "industrial heritage." Although this might address some of the concerns about the exclusion of particular narratives and an unrepresentative version of the past, she notes that "industrial ruins are problematic public spaces due to the complex range of issues and emotions they can invoke" (p. 90).

Smith (2006) addresses these concerns by declaring that "there is no such thing as heritage," by which she means that it cannot be regarded as an uncontested truth; she proposes, rather, that we view it not as an object but "as a cultural and social process, which engages with acts of remembering that work to create ways to understand and engage with the present" (p. 2). It is the present-day cultural activities that these objects are part of that gives them meaning, she contends. In this account of heritage, the present is as significant as the past and Smith (p. 3) argues against a notion of "inherent cultural value or significance" to artifacts. For Smith, heritage can be seen as both the practice of the heritage industry and a cultural practice in identity making.

Heritage, then, can be seen as fulfilling an important role of preservation, preventing many buildings from falling into disrepair and artworks from entering private collections. It is not a politically neutral approach, however, and what merits "saving" in heritage terms, in what condition, and how this is presented in relation to current society are all contentious issues. This is particularly so when heritage relates to national identity, as it so often does.

Heritage and national identity are closely aligned, as Harrison (2010) argues, through the construction of an agreed canon of art. This canon "might be understood to represent ideological tools that circulate the values on which particular visions of nationhood are established" (p. 15). The collection of objects—be they buildings, paintings, sculptures, or monuments—is considered part of the canon because these objects express the values that culture wishes to promote and the narratives central to the notion of nationhood. Canetti (1962) argues that "crowd symbols" are significant in constructing national shared values. For England, they suggest, the sea is a crowd symbol, whereas for France it is the French Revolution, and perhaps for Wales mountains play a similar role. These crowd symbols are more significant than history or territory, and they represent common, well-understood symbols, which could sustain a popular feeling of nationhood. The heritage canon, then, can be seen as a means of manifesting these crowd symbols in the form of artifacts.

What constitutes national identity is often a complex issue, however, that goes beyond these crowd symbols. Anderson (2006, p. 3) notes that "nation, nationality, nationalism—all have proved notoriously difficult to define, let alone to analyse." This is frustrating for those involved in the heritage industry since nationality is both entirely an "imagined community" and a persistent and strong identifier for many people. Anderson argues that it is best viewed as a cultural artifact. But this is perhaps to underplay its resilience and significance. To be useful, then, a concept of nationhood as it relates to art must be rooted in some aspect of everyday life.

It is perhaps a sense of identity that heritage appeals to when we consider nationhood. If nationality is viewed at least in part as an issue of identity, then Mead (1934) suggests that an individual's identity is created by the degree to which that person absorbs the values of their community, summarized in the phrase "self reflects society." Snow (2001) also argues that identity is largely constructed socially and includes, as well as Mead's sense of belonging, a sense of difference from other communities. Identity is seen as a shared sense of "we-ness" developed through shared attributes and experiences and in contrast to one or more sets of others. National identity, then, is both an imagined and a real community, with a strong sense of everyday validity to many. It can be seen as representing the stories that we tell about ourselves, and heritage is the tool for framing those stories.

Turning now to ed tech, by attempting to frame it as an undiscipline, or something less rigorously bounded than a discipline, practitioners within it seek to avoid the museumification process identified above. A discipline can be seen as analogous to a museum, seeking to curate the works, methods, and figures that represent the core artifacts or canon. This canon involves the use of gatekeepers who decide what is worthy of inclusion, just as the heritage industry determines which buildings are worthy of preservation. This process inevitably has a backward-looking emphasis, and for good reason it is resistant to change, as Kuhn's theory of paradigm shifts argues. However, in an area such as ed tech, this process might not be appropriate. It is too multidisciplinary, so in effect it is a series of museums, and it is more in a state of flux, so the process of heritage is not deeply rooted. However, as with national identity, there is an identity among ed tech practitioners, some shared crowd symbols, and common values. This identity is both meaningful and entirely imagined, just like national identity.

One solution, therefore, is to look for examples of institutions that have sought to address the issue of museumification and remain dynamic while reflecting identity and helping to engage in a constructive dialogue on what that identity means. One such example is the Museum of Welsh Life, in St Fagans, near Cardiff. It has a specific remit to reflect the everyday lives of Welsh people. It is an open-air museum (the first such in Britain), featuring buildings of Wales from the Iron Age to the

1960s. There are over 40 buildings, which have been either relocated from other sites in Wales or reconstructed, including houses, a farm, a school, a chapel, and a Workmen's Institute. The museum focuses on representing typical buildings, rather than exceptional or unique ones, since it seeks to represent all aspects of Welsh life.

As such, it can be seen as a direct reaction to notions of national identity shaped around paintings or exceptional works or the lives of the elite. Mason (2005, p. 22) suggests that the museum "operates as a space in which it is possible to identify competing definitions of Welshness."

By representing everyday life in an outdoor setting, the museum seeks to create a view across different aspects of Welsh identity. In ed tech, this can be replicated by turning away from the deification of individuals in technology (e.g., Steve Jobs as a role model) and instead focusing on what might be termed more everyday artifacts or, in this case, practical benefits for learners. The more open approach allows for a constant dialogue on what it means to be an educational technologist. For example, when the Museum of Modern Life unveiled a restored church, St Teilo's, it recovered original wall paintings from before the Reformation. They were bright and graphic, depicting scenes from the Passion for an illiterate audience. However, they did not match modern sensibilities about what a church in Wales looked like, with its strong Methodist tradition. This led to debate about the true identity of Welshness, which was largely positive. Similarly, an approach in ed tech that encourages reflection on what it means to engage in educational technology is generally useful in moving the area forward. For instance, when Watters (2019) published a list of a decade of ed tech failures, many found it a useful reminder and check, whereas others wondered about the inclusion or omission of some entries, and still others wanted a counter-list of successes. We can view this kind of work as a form of dialogue-inducing curation, which—like St Teilo's church—allows people to position themselves in relation to it. Maintaining a perspective that actively resists museumification while recognizing the importance and shifting nature of identity can be used to generate such artifacts and promote the discussion about them.

Digital Mudlarking

The final metaphor for the consideration of ed tech as an undiscipline is that of mudlarking. Wikipedia describes a mudlark as "someone who scavenges in river mud for items of value, a term used especially to describe those who scavenged this way in London during the late 18th and 19th centuries" (Wikipedia, 2021).

I was enamoured of the stories that my mother, a Cockney, told me of growing up using the Thames as a beach, playground, and treasure trove, so I have always found the idea of mudlarks intriguing. Mudlarks have a decidedly Dickensian feel, but we should not let the romantic images detract from the dangerous reality, an unhealthy and risky pursuit undertaken by the poorest of children for meagre returns.

Mudlarking has seen something of a modern-day revival, particularly with the advent of metal detectors. Maiklem (2019) provides a detailed account of the life of the modern mudlarker, and there are some resonances in what she describes with ed tech as a discipline.

As mentioned above, one of the elements of ed tech that makes the idea of a discipline an ill fit is that it does not have the foundations of other disciplines. People come to it from different fields, what it actually is might not be clearly defined, and there is no shared sense of history. So, thinking about a history of ed tech is less akin to the archaeological dig that one might undertake in other fields since there is no agreed boundary for what such an excavation should cover or even what the artifacts worth recovering would be. It is also very dynamic and constantly in flux, like conducting such a dig in sand. If you are an ed tech practitioner, then, the sense is less of an excavation and more of hurried gathering and acquisition. Ed tech practitioners can be seen to operate like mudlarks, gathering artifacts that have been exposed by the last tide of technology. These artifacts can be seen as examples of good practice, pertinent research, or useful concepts that have applications across different technologies. Examples might be approaches to support learners at a distance, effective methods to encourage online dialogue, frameworks for ethics of application, and so on.

Consider, for example, that over the past 20 years we have witnessed initial elearning interest, the web 2.0 bubble, rapid interest in

MOOCs, current hype about AI, application of data, and the online pivot as substantial trends in ed tech. We can view each of them as a tide, depositing knowledge artifacts that will be washed away by the next big wave unless they are carefully gathered and restored by the digital mudlarks. After each of these waves, there is a space momentarily revealed where reflection and research can be found. These artifacts are shaped by the tide but have value and currency independently. I argued in *25 Years of Ed Tech* (Weller, 2020) that one of the problems with ed tech as a field is that it does not value its own history. In this metaphor, it pays attention only to each new tide, so these contributions are forgotten or lost.

This became evident during the online pivot when a number of articles appeared declaring the ineffectiveness of online learning. For example, Rayment-Pickard (2020) argued that online education worked against widening participation. There were the usual claims about the mystique of face-to-face lectures. Zimmerman (2020), for example, claimed that remote learning led to the death of charisma. Supiano (2020) asked "Can You Create Learning Communities Online?" Although useful advice was offered, that it was posed as a question—as if it had never been realized previously—was telling about the lack of penetration that online learning has realized in the mainstream.

Many such articles exhibited an ignorance of the preceding 20 years of online learning and 50 years of distance education. This is where the digital mudlarkers can reveal their treasures. For example, the first thing to note is that online learning traditionally has served a different audience. It has affordances different from those of face-to-face learning, particularly in allowing learners to partake asynchronously and structure their learning according to their own convenience and preference. Having an appreciation of knowledge acquired from previous waves of ed tech helps individuals and institutions to frame their responses in circumstances such as the online pivot.

Metaphors are also interesting when they do not quite fit and offer some insight into this mismatch. For example, one aspect of this mudlarking metaphor to be cautious about is the connotation of a tide. This plays into notions of technological change as inevitable and irresistible. We could argue that it is our job to shape the direction or flow of the tide as much as to gather what is deposited, but I would add that as a practitioner it sometimes does *feel* like a tide—you have little say, for instance, in whether your institution is going to adopt MOOCs.

Overall, though, educational technologists need to ensure that value can be gathered from each of these waves and that it is preserved and shared. Maiklem (2019) posits that mudlarking is a skill that took time and patience, requiring many fruitless hours in the Thames mud before she developed the appropriate skills, which is referred to as 'getting your eye in' by mudlarkers. The skill to spot objects of interest amid the general detritus can also be said to be a defining characteristic of the educational technologist—it takes time to get "your eye in" and appreciate what is important and useful in new technological developments and to separate them from the pro- or anti-technology rhetoric.

CHAPTER 4

Specific Ed Tech

The previous two chapters can be seen as refining the focus of this book. Having established some foundational context for the internet and associated metaphors, and then considered the nature of the "undiscipline" that constitutes ed tech, I can now turn to some metaphors related to specific educational technologies. This type of metaphor is probably the most prevalent and arguably the most useful. It can help us to frame our reactions to new technologies and to place them within our own mental constructs. Of course, many technologies come wrapped in their own metaphors—an eportfolio, for instance, has the immediate analogy of a physical portfolio, such as an artist, architect, or designer might develop. Computer interfaces made strong use of metaphors such as the desktop, filing cabinet, and wastepaper bin. Early online communication spaces, the forerunners of much of today's social media, were called electronic bulletin board systems, with the metaphor of a physical bulletin board onto which people can pin different notices. Such metaphors provide cognitive scaffolding, helping users to convey models of behaviour from their existing, familiar practices, for example putting trash in the bin. They can also be limiting in that users can take the metaphors too literally or map incorrect elements across domains. For example, the bin metaphor on the computer desktop was useful to simplify the rather obscure method of freeing up memory that could be overwritten, but it also gave people overconfidence that files were actually destroyed, and it was confusingly used to eject disks in the Mac OS for a while (Theus & Interkom, 1999).

In this chapter, I propose four metaphors related to specific educational technologies. The first uses the application of video-assisted refereeing (VAR) in football (soccer) to think about learning analytics. Both technologies force us to confront the essentially human nature of the enterprise to which they are applied. In the next section, I cover the much-hyped technology of blockchain, in particular the desire of its devotees to offer a magical solution to all problems, which has a resonance with the practice of alchemy. In the section on MOOCs, I offer two metaphors. MOOCs encouraged much debate around 2012, often couched in terms of metaphors. They represent the prime example of a recent ed tech wave (as described in the previous chapter) that many people struggled to place in an appropriate perspective. Were they the end of universities as we knew them or largely irrelevant? The answer to this question often depended on the metaphors with which they were presented. In the last section of this chapter, I address the most prevalent ed tech, namely the LMS or VLE. The LMS has been very successful, and a number of different metaphors have been applied to its implementation, dominance, and pedagogical model.

VAR and Learning Analytics

Although higher education and professional sports are obviously different worlds, both ed tech and video-assisted refereeing are concerned with the application of technology to fundamentally human enterprises, with the intention of improving them for those involved. Witnessing the rollout of the VAR technology at the men's and women's Football World Cup tournaments in 2018 and 2019, and in the UK Premier League for the 2019–20 season, provided some possible lessons for the application of technology in education, in particular the use of large data sets to analyze student behaviour.

Let's examine first the history of VAR. In 2012, the Royal Netherlands Football Association (KNVB) set about trying to use technology to improve decision making in the game with a project called Refereeing 2.0 (KNVB, n.d.). In the 2013–14 season, it piloted the use of technology such as Hawk Eye, which had already been deployed successfully in cricket, to assess whether a ball had fully crossed the goal line. The pilot also developed the use of fifth and sixth officials who could examine video evidence and communicate with the on-pitch referees.

With detailed television coverage and mobile phone footage from the crowd, the use of video to support the referee in football seemed to be inevitable. As the president of the International Football Association (responsible for the rules of the game) put it, "with all the 4G and Wi-Fi in stadia today, the referee is the only person who can't see exactly what is happening and he's actually the only one who should" (qtd. in Medeiros, 2018). It was hard to argue against the implementation of video technology when every refereeing decision was being dissected in minute detail via television and social media. VAR had good intentions, namely, to eliminate an increasing number of obvious errors. The technology involves the use of video footage analyzed by the video assistant referee in a separate video suite. That referee relays information back to the on-field officials. The technology is now in use across most professional leagues, although the exact guidance on when and how it is used can vary.

On a positive note, there are aspects of VAR that really do help and have improved the overall game. Goal line technology, for instance, has removed the infuriating experience of disallowed goals when a ball has clearly crossed the line. However, the intersection of precise technology with dynamic and imprecise activity in football has led to incidents in which the technology provides a false sense of confidence about aspects not reducible to minute measurements. VAR decisions in which a ball has brushed a hair on someone's hand and is deemed a handball, or in which a player is ruled offside by a fingertip, might be correct technically, but in reality the game and the rules were not developed to be so finely measured. Fans are increasingly frustrated as a seemingly good goal is subjected to forensic analysis and eventually disallowed. The application of such fine measurement to a human enterprise seems to be a mismatch, like using molecular changes in the brain to describe poetry. It can be done, but it rather misses the point. As Farry (2020) puts it, "football has always been a game defined as much by human error . . . [as] by human skill," and VAR threatens that dynamic.

Turning to learning analytics in education, we can see a number of parallels. Learning analytics can be defined as "the measurement, collection, analysis, and reporting of data about learners and their contexts, for the purposes of understanding and optimizing learning and the environments in which it occurs" (Siemens, 2013, p. 1382). Because students spend a good deal of time in virtual environments, and because most education systems (e.g., the library, attendance, and student records) generate data about them, HEIs now possess a wealth of precise data about a student. It can include how long they spend looking at a resource, the number and average length of posts that they put on an online forum, their performance across computer-based assessments, how often they access library resources, and so on. This quantity of data can lead us to believe that we can measure a student's comprehension of a subject to a fine degree, but as with football learning is much more inexact than the measurements might suggest. As with VAR, we can be misled into thinking that the precise measurement is significant rather than the overall quality. As with obvious errors in VAR, possessing rich and accurate data can better inform our decisions, but they need to be implemented sympathetically with a holistic view of the enterprise (be that football or education).

Another point of comparison is that VAR forces us to re-evaluate the role of humans in the system. Arguably, the application of technology in cricket has been more advantageous, with Hawk Eye and an established video review system to support increasingly complex decisions for umpires. Here the technology is implemented within a framework in which its role is to support the human decision makers. Similarly, learning analytics can be used to help an educator identify whether a student is struggling, whether a particularly tough part of a course is causing students to revisit materials often, or whether certain resources are not being used. In the online course delivery world, this type of data is the equivalent of detecting puzzled faces, stifled yawns, or stares out the window during a lecture, and the educator can make adjustments accordingly. As with VAR, though, there is the danger that learning analytics make the data the most important aspect, and that the decision could be made by an AI system, just as teaching could be deemed a task for AI. Implementing technology with the aim to support rather than replace actors in the field is a key principle that we can extract.

With VAR, we are also seeing how the technology changes the behaviour of humans who make decisions. If referees and umpires know that video technology will catch misdemeanours, then maybe they will be less likely to give fouls, or maybe they will trust their own judgment less. Johnson (2020) reports that by January 2 in the UK Premier League 2019–20 season a total of 63 refereeing decisions had been overturned by VAR. This was bound to have an effect on the people whose decisions were publicly reversed in this manner. Similarly, an educator might not trust their own judgment about a student if the technology tells them otherwise and if they know that they are being monitored on the basis of the data. A possible consequence of the quantity of data mentioned previously is that only data-driven decisions are trusted.

Perhaps most tellingly, much like a lot of ed tech, including learning analytics, VAR has not really solved the problems that it set out to eliminate, at least in the manner that people envisaged. Football fans are now in the strange position of thinking that VAR is ruining the game but do not want it scrapped. There was an increasing desire for video technology to be applied to football to solve incorrect offside decisions, missed penalty calls, and goals that should have been disallowed. The belief was that, if video-assisted refereeing was in use, then all of these problems would disappear. The introduction of VAR alleviated some of these complaints, but it also introduced a whole new set of issues, so now there are arguments about whether decisions should have been referred to VAR and whether the fine calls mentioned above should have been given. The debate has just moved the location from the pitch to the review room. Football games are still not the controversy-free utopia that many envisaged, and arguments about and dissatisfaction with rulings have probably only increased.

It is difficult, then, to say ultimately that the introduction of VAR has been worthwhile. Similarly, in education, the introduction of technology such as MOOCs, AI, or blockchain is often touted as solving problems of equity, access, scale, or efficiency. For instance, MOOCs were meant to democratize education by making courses free to all. But the lack of tutor support in a MOOC has meant that it is best suited to experienced, confident learners. This is indeed what a demographic analysis of MOOC learners has revealed (Christensen et al., 2013), with the result that, far from democratizing education, MOOCs might actually increase inequality. Although most forms of ed tech find a suitable audience and purpose, invariably they cost more than anticipated and do not have the global impacts touted at their inception.

VAR highlights that we should view technology as part of a broader system. It is likely that the implementation of VAR will improve, but that will happen not through technological development but through a more sympathetic and nuanced set of guidelines for its usage. The same is true of learning analytics and other implementations of ed tech. The technology needs to be understood as part of the wider educational context and not a solution in itself.

Overall, though VAR improves some decisions, there is the possibility that it dehumanizes aspects of football. Our enjoyment in watching a sport is precisely that it is not an exact science: it is unpredictable, sometimes chaotic, and conducted by people. That is what makes it worth returning to. Technology can certainly improve it, but its application needs to be cautious, and our expectations for its results need to be measured, for it will not lead to a sporting nirvana devoid of errors. Accepting the messiness of sport is part of its inherent appeal, and so it is with education. Although education is more controllable and perhaps predictable, it is still an exploit that we undertake because it connects to some very human aspect of self and identity. As with VAR, the role of technology in education is largely inevitable—we are not returning to a time without ubiquitous video in sport or one without the internet in education. It can also be potentially beneficial; however, as we are seeing with video technology in sport, it is to the detriment of the overall enterprise if it becomes the main focus.

Blockchain and Alchemy

Few technologies have excited as much attention without having a direct application for most people as "blockchain." It seemed that there was no problem to which blockchain was not the solution. In this section, I examine this form of techno-solutionism and why blockchain represents a type of technology attractive to many.

But first some explanation of the technology. A blockchain is formed from a database shared across a network of computers. The network is public but encrypted, so when an update is made to the database, such as a new transaction, it is automatically updated across the network. This distributed nature makes it difficult to hack since any hacker would need to make changes across the network. Cryptocurrencies such as Bitcoin use blockchain to create a ledger that holds the records of Bitcoin transactions. The lack of a central location storing this database makes it secure and ideal for online, peer-to-peer transactions.

Around 2017, people began to suggest that it could have applications in education. In a review of its possible applications in education, Grech and Camilleri (2017) proposed four possible areas of impact:

1. A system for certification: records of achievement could be securely stored via blockchain and expanded to include credit transfer and recognition of informal learning.

2. Verification of validity: users can automatically check the validity of certificates without the need to contact the organizations that originally issued them.

3. Ownership of data: users could have increased ownership of and control over their own data, which would reduce data management costs for universities.

4. Cryptocurrency payments: institutions and individuals can use cryptocurrency payment methods, which could enhance grant or voucher-based funding models.

Similarly, Fagan (2018) reported on several university pilots and start-ups experimenting with blockchain approaches for credentialing and recognizing competency-based achievements, and the University of Bahrain announced that it was using blockchain to provide all students with a digital record of achievement (Galea-Pace, 2019).

Beyond these rather niche applications, there is a broader tendency to promote blockchain as a mystical solution to all manner of problems. For instance, in 2018, Chancellor of the Exchequer of the United Kingdom Phillip Hammond suggested that it was the means to solve the potential border issue with Ireland should the United Kingdom leave the European Union: "I don't claim to be an expert on it but the most obvious technology is blockchain" (quoted in Cellan-Jones, 2018, para. 3). How blockchain would solve this problem and far larger social ones was not made clear. It was a magical solution.

Maintaining this aura of magic is not accidental. Blockchain, after all, is a solution that will be sold by providers, and transparency and understanding are not always in their interests. In an analysis of 43 blockchain applications, Burg et al. (2018, para. 5) found "no documentation or evidence of the results blockchain was purported to have achieved." None of the reported solutions was willing to share data, results, or processes. The authors concluded that, "despite all the hype about how blockchain will bring unheralded transparency to processes and operations in low-trust environments, the industry is itself opaque" (para. 6).

Blockchain can be seen as the latest instantiation of a recurring theme in ed tech that can be termed "technology as alchemy." "Alchemy" is a term often used to imply a magical solution, and a search for its application in scholarly articles reveals titles such as "Genetic Alchemy," "The Alchemy of Finance," "Computational Alchemy," and "The Alchemy of Asset Securitization." It is used loosely and metaphorically in most of these instances to imply a beneficial but secret and mysterious process of transmutation that is part science and part art. Holmyard (1990) divides alchemy into two parts: exoteric, concerned with preparing or discovering the philosopher's stone, with its power of transmuting base metals into precious ones, and esoteric, devotion and mystical practice that lead to eternal life and in which the transmutation of base metals is merely symbolic (although no doubt convenient).

There is much that is interesting in the history of alchemy, including its origins in ancient China, its relations to Christianity and Islam, its influence on literature (Shakespeare and Chaucer made references to alchemy as well as its presence in the Harry Potter series), and the modelling of an early ecological thinking (Wilson et al., 2007). All of these perspectives, and many more, make alchemy a topic of interest in its own right. However, this analogy focuses on a more negative interpretation and its relation to the history of chemistry. The pursuit of unlimited precious metals in particular dominated experimentation in chemistry for centuries and reappeared in different cultures and at different times. Although it had mystical and religious elements for many, the dogged pursuit of alchemy was also characterized by the following:

- Greed: unlimited wealth awaited the successful alchemist.

- Obfuscation: alchemy persisted through rumour and secret formulas, adding to its allure. The process was never made public.

- Magical lexicon: this obfuscation worked not only by being secretive but also by creating a language difficult to penetrate.

- Vagueness: although the ultimate aim of producing gold was clear, it was accompanied by vagueness regarding other benefits, including immortality, spiritual awakening, and improved health.

- Occasional side benefits: almost inevitably, given the time devoted to it, there was the occasional chemical breakthrough that occurred as a side benefit of alchemy, such as the discovery of phosphorus.

- Persistence despite the lack of results: although there was no success in transmuting base metals into gold, people persisted, and indeed this complete lack of success was only seen as a reason to continue. Succeeding where others had failed represented an irresistible challenge, and some of the best scientific minds (e.g., Isaac Newton) were involved in this largely fruitless pursuit.

Although blockchain is not as elusive as alchemy, there are similarities to how it is sold and portrayed. Blockchain is by no means alone in employing an alchemical mindset in its promotion—proponents of AI, learning analytics, and automatic assessment can all be said to deploy similar tactics. From the perspective of blockchain, we can consider the similarities to the list of aspects of alchemy:

- Greed: the global education market is estimated at $6 trillion annually, and selling a universal solution across all providers linked to their most treasured asset (accreditation) would provide significant returns.

- Obfuscation: it is frequently made obscure by commercial interests with black box algorithms. As the study above highlights, they report questionable results that are difficult to verify and do not share their data.

- Magical lexicon: it has its own lexicon of algorithms, ledgers, and encryption that increasingly looks like magic to outsiders.

- Vagueness: there is often a vagueness about improved efficiency, learner agency, lifelong learning, and so on. The four potential impacts suggested by Grech and Camilleri (2017) indicate some of these ill-defined possible benefits, such as improved efficiency in institutions' data management systems.

- Side benefits: perhaps not accidental, but amid all of the investment, it is likely that there will be some practical advantages of blockchain that will be over-reported. For example, instant access to trusted digital certificates without the need to contact institutions will benefit refugees whose original paper certificates might have been lost or destroyed.

- Persistence: Watters (2013a) talked of "zombie ideas" in ed tech that just refuse to die. Automatic tuition and micro-credentialing are among these ideas, and blockchain represents the latest technology to offer solutions for them.

This is not to suggest that blockchain cannot be successfully implemented and possibly solve specific issues that provide real benefits for learners. The objection here is to the overblown claims and the often-unspoken alchemical tradition that persists in ed tech, of which blockchain is merely the latest realization. The effective way to combat this is through openness (of data, algorithms, claims, and results), focusing on specific problems to address (instead of grand revolutions) and bringing a critical perspective to any "magical" solution.

The alchemical tradition is founded partly upon a lack of transparency and partly upon being a new, complete solution. Such approaches therefore exhibit the type of historical amnesia that besets much of ed tech. For instance, DeMillo (2019) writes about "How Blockchain Technology Will Disrupt Higher Education": "It will do so by solving a problem that few of us realized we had: There is no reliably efficient and consistent way to keep track of a person's entire educational history. That is why a worldwide effort is underway to use blockchain technology to tame the internet so that it can become a universal, permanent record of educational achievement." This is in fact a problem that many people in education recognized and indeed one that they thought they had solved with eportfolios. The benefit of blockchain, DeMillo claims, is that it will open up what we recognize as assessment: "Students are more than transcripts and test scores. The college transcript is a 19th-century invention that has little to do with the educational institutions and workplaces of the 21st century."

We can compare this with how Beetham (2005, p. 3) summarized the benefits of an eportfolio, which

- provide evidence of an individual's progress and achievements

- [are] drawn from both formal and informal learning activities

- are personally managed and owned by the learner

- can be used for review, reflection, and personal development planning

- can be selectively accessed by other interested parties, e.g., teachers, peers, assessors, awarding bodies, prospective employers.

That has a lot of resonance with what DeMillo (2019) says that block-chain can deliver. Arguably, eportfolios have not been as successful as they could have been, but some of the issues in their uptake are related not to the technology but to the context within which they operate. For instance, employers generally *say* that they would like to have a complete portfolio of an applicant's work, but they tend to fall back on CVs and interviews. Similarly, eportfolios require assessment in universities to be reshaped so that they are based upon discrete tasks more usefully added as stand-alone pieces of evidence.

Blockchain might represent a better way of achieving this result, but an article declaring how it will change the method of assessment should at least acknowledge the existence of eportfolios. The questions that it should be answering are how will blockchain do it better, and how will it overcome the problems that a decade or more of eportfolio work has not managed to address? The problem with an alchemical mindset is that these questions seem to be mundane compared with the fantastical offering proposed.

As with alchemy, the danger of blockchain is that there will be wasted time, effort, and money in the pursuit of an unattainable goal instead of focusing on smaller, achievable ones. In alchemy, once experimenters stopped trying to produce gold, they went on to discover elements, invent medicines, and create all manner of new materials that could be used every day. As educational technologists, then, we should always be wary of any technology that has the whiff of alchemy about it, and the traits above provide a useful checklist against which to review any technological solution.

MOOC Metaphors

Massive open online courses can be regarded as the educational technology that garnered the most interest over the past decade, starting with experiments by the likes of George Siemens and Stephen Downes; seeing large-scale investment and media attention, with 2012 being declared the year of the MOOC (Pappano, 2012); engaging in a wealth of associated research (Veletsianos & Shepherdson, 2016); and settling into more practical forms of application. As such, they also attracted a lot of metaphorical thinking as people struggled to understand what they were in relation to conventional higher education. Were MOOCs education's "MP3" (Shirky, 2012), broadcast (McAndrew & Scanlon, 2013), rhizomes (Cormier, 2008), or a shop window (Wakefield et al., 2018)? I will consider two metaphors, one from Downes and one of my own, as a means of exploring how metaphors help us to think about a new technology.

Uncle MOOC

The main innovation (if one wants to label it as such) that Uber offered was the avoidance of obligations to employees and meeting labour regulations. In a similar way, some of the excitement about MOOCs stemmed from their ability to bypass much of the regulation and responsibility inherent in a formal education system.

The first bypass was the removal of student supports, including tutors, assessment and feedback, helpdesks, et cetera. From the experience of the UKOU and other distance education institutions, it is well known that support is the costliest element of a course, largely because it is a variable cost that increases as the number of students increases. Course production is a fixed cost in that it costs roughly as much to produce a course if one person or 100,000 people study it. Therefore, if you remove the substantial costs of support, then it is possible to offer courses cheaply. However, support is necessary if you want reasonable completion rates and a learner demographic that does not benefit experienced learners.

These support services are key to long-term success for learners, but their uptake is not evenly distributed. Some learners hardly ever avail themselves of such services, they don't care about tuition, and they do very well studying on their own. Other learners require a lot of support for various reasons and probably use more than their "fair" share of these services (i.e., more than they have actually paid for). Most students are in the middle and make use of them sometimes, depending on circumstances. The first group, the confident, independent learners, tend to do well in MOOCs. They probably represent the 10% or so who complete them. Then there are some students for whom no amount of support can help them; either study is not for them, or the time is wrong. But in the middle is a substantial number of students who need varying levels of support to complete a protracted course of study. If MOOC dropout over seven weeks is 90%, then imagine what it would be like over 3 or 4 years of degree study. Support is the crucial factor in helping to retain students at this level of study.

The alternatives to such costly models of support are automation through artificial intelligence, "pay as you use it" tutor support, and community or peer support. They can go some way toward alleviating the demands on support but are unlikely to replace them completely. Therefore, MOOCs simply abandon a large proportion of potential learners with a sink-or-swim approach. This is not a sustainable or desirable model for a global education system.

MOOCs are also often portrayed as a response to the rising cost of university education (e.g., Ruth, 2014). One of the common complaints about rising university costs is the increased cost of administrative staff. This is usually portrayed as greed or university laziness; for instance, Belkin and Thurm (2012) reported a 37% increase in admin staff from 2001 to 2012. Kiley (2011) accused HEIs of wastefulness: "They waste a lot of money on redundant administrative activities and could probably save money in the long run if they made big changes to their structure." And Erdley (2013) revealed that administrative spending in universities in Pennsylvania increased 53% from 2001 to 2010.

The general argument of these articles is that it is simply avarice, or unnecessary bureaucracy, that has led to this situation, with the implicit suggestion that, if universities were "proper" businesses, they wouldn't succumb to such wastefulness. As with support, MOOCs seemingly offer one way to provide an education without all of this unnecessary administrative cost. One of the common complaints can be paraphrased as "universities used to be more efficient and not need as many admin staff." The second part is true, universities did not need as many admin staff in the past, but that was largely because the amount of legislation that universities had to respond to was far less. Consider the following areas, all of which affect universities, and ask whether the associated administration related to them has increased or decreased over the past 30 years:

- student accessibility and widening participation

- financial accountability, tax, charity status

- health and safety

- estates and property

- international students and business

- student recruitment, teaching quality assessment, pastoral care

- research bidding and reporting

- employment law

A university nowadays has a large, complex administration because it operates in a large, complex environment, probably far more so than most companies that have particular focuses and are concerned with legislation that relates only to their niche practices. In the 1970s, only one administrator in a department was necessary because there was not the associated legislation. Any university operating such a laissez-faire approach now would be shut down or face criminal charges for failing to respond appropriately to legislation.

The question, then, is not so much "why do universities spend so much on admin?" but "do we want society to make universities spend this much on admin?" And here people can be a bit hypocritical—they will probably be in favour of reducing the admin spend but then demand robust appeal procedures or sue a university for not taking due care. These are issues beyond universities, and society cannot place an increasingly complex legislative and administrative burden on universities and then complain that they spend more money on legislative and administrative tasks. MOOCs can eschew much of this spend precisely because universities exist to realize much of it, but if they are to be the replacement for university education then they would be forced to adopt it.

To come to our metaphor, MOOCs are akin to the patronizing uncle who has yet to have a child of his own. Uncles are great fun for nieces and nephews, they are inventive and playful, and the children always look forward to their arrival. But the uncle secretly thinks that he could do a better job at raising the children than their parents. The uncle might also think that the children prefer him to their mom and dad. "Why don't they do all the stuff I do with them?" he might think. "I'm great at getting them out of a tantrum, I do my distraction technique, and they forget it. I never see their dad doing that," he compliments himself. "I would have a set of rules that the kids would respect and obey, not this slapdash approach," he vows. And then, of course, he has children of his own. Suddenly, he realizes that he has to work as well as raise kids, that the distraction techniques do not work with a tired 6-month-old at 3 a.m., and that getting the basic stuff done every day, such as feeding, bathing, and looking after them, is a real achievement in itself.

This is how MOOCs and their relationship with formal education can be viewed. They are good fun, they offer something new, and a lot of learners really enjoy them. But they should not fool themselves that they can do the robust, day-to-day stuff better and more cheaply than the existing system. If they had to, then they would soon find that a lot of their energy is spent on the mundane matters, because that is required of them.

MOOCs and Newspapers

One of the issues with MOOCs that quickly became apparent was their low completion rate. If MOOCs were to be the revolution in higher education, then this claim is undermined when only about 10% of learners complete a MOOC (Lewin, 2013). Jordan (2014) plotted completion rates using various sources of publicly available data. The average completion rate (and there are different ways of defining completion) was 12.6%. A study by the University of Pennsylvania found lower completion rates of around 6% (Perna et al., 2014). There is usually considerable drop-off after week 1, with some number of active learners usually consistent by about week 3. The pattern of steep decline in active users seems to be consistent across all disciplines.

Others have argued that course completion is the wrong way to view success in MOOCs. Anderson et al. (2014) suggest that talking about "drop-outs" in MOOCs misses a more fine-grained taxonomy of behaviours. They propose five categories:

1. viewers who primarily watch lectures;

2. solvers who primarily hand in assignments for a grade;

3. all-rounders who balance the watching of lectures with the handing in of assignments;

4. collectors who primarily download lectures; and

5. bystanders who registered for the course but whose activity is very minimal.

However, across six courses, bystanders usually account for 50% and viewers a further 20%, representing a lot of non-active learners even in their more generous interpretation of MOOC learner behaviour.

The commonly used argument against completion rates is that they are not relevant. Downes (2014) proposes that taking a MOOC is more like reading a newspaper; we don't say that someone has "dropped out" of a newspaper, since they just read in it what they want: "People don't read a newspaper to complete it, they read a newspaper to find out what's important." This analogy is appealing, but it is really a statement of intent. MOOCs could be designed to be newspaper-like, and then the MOOC experience could be like reading a newspaper. But the vast majority of MOOCs are not designed that way. And, even for those that are, completion rates are still an issue.

MOOCs are nearly always designed on a week-by-week basis, which would be like designing a newspaper in which you have to read a certain section by a certain time. About 45% of those who sign up for a MOOC never turn up or do anything at all. It is hard to argue that they have a meaningful learning experience. So let us take those who are active in some way as the starting point, even if it is just looking at the first page of the course. By the end of week 2, the total number of active users is down to about 35% of initial registrations, and by week 3 or 4 it has plateaued at about 10%. The data suggest that people definitely do not treat a MOOC like a newspaper. In Japan (Japan Guide

2001), some research was done on what sections of newspapers people read. There is an interesting gender split, but the sections are evenly divided. The percentage shows the proportion of readers who read a particular section, but they usually read more than one section. For men, the top five sections were as follows:

- headlines (62.0%)

- domestic news (55.4%)

- sports (55.4%)

- economy (53.3%)

- international news (47.8%)

For women, the top five sections were as follows:

- TV listings (71.4%)

- headlines (65.3%)

- domestic news (53.3%)

- international news (50.8%)

- crimes and accidents (39.2%)

If MOOCs are like newspapers, then you would expect a similar pattern, with roughly equal numbers across different weeks, say 65% to read the topics in week 1 and 54% the topics in week 7. This doesn't happen. It could happen if MOOCs were designed that way and if you thought that it was appropriate for your subject matter. But to say that it does happen is simply incorrect. To reverse the analogy from Downes, if newspapers are like MOOCs, then 50% would read the headlines, but only about 10% would get to the sports. The differences in these distributions illustrate why the analogy is inappropriate.

Now, for individuals this might not matter, they have studied as far as they want, and maybe it has been a meaningful experience (or a painful experience because they have felt out of their depth). But for MOOCs in general, as a learning approach, it really does matter. Many MOOCs are about 6–7 weeks long, so 90% of the registered learners never get to see approximately 50% of the content. That should raise the question of why it is included in the first place. For this reason, many providers recommend that MOOCs be only 4 weeks long; for instance, most FutureLearn courses are about that length. But that limits what can be covered in many subjects and seems to be like abandoning a topic before too many students drop out. If a MOOC is like a newspaper, then longer MOOCs are preferable since they give people more areas to choose from, like the different sections of a newspaper. For many MOOC vendors, it is in their commercial interests to dismiss drop-out rates as irrelevant, but I would suggest that, when vendors claim that completion rates don't matter, it is worth considering whether they would still make that claim if they had 90% completion rates.

These metaphors regarding MOOCs reveal that they presented a challenge to how education interacted with the internet, even if they were not as new or revolutionary as many proclaimed. They are a prime example of how metaphors are used to frame a technology, and to discuss the issues with it, for good and ill.

VLE/LMS

The virtual learning environment (VLE) or learning management system (LMS)—largely synonymous, with LMS favoured in the North American context—is in many ways the default educational technology. It grew out of the elearning boom at the end of the 1990s, when many institutions were deploying a mixture of technologies to implement online learning. An online course back then might have combined websites for content, a third-party tool for computer conferencing, in-house tools for submitting assignments, an open-source piece of software for quizzes, and so on. Although this range of options meant that the environment could be tailored to the educator's needs, pedagogical requirements, or just simple preferences, it could be confusing for students navigating different configurations across multiple courses. Also, setting up and working with these various tools required both a certain degree of technical knowledge (even to have conversations with IT people who might do the hard work) and an interest in doing so. Many academics, justifiably, are just not interested in ed tech; they have their own domain knowledge to focus on, and ed tech can be a distraction or impediment.

Enter the VLE, which provided a neat collection of the most popular tools in one package, with a uniform interface, and links to other university systems, such as registration, student records, the library, and content management. This enabled a consistent experience for students across the university, uniform staff development, and centralized IT support. By the mid-2000s, the VLE was a mainstream part of nearly every university's infrastructure. Its rise was dramatic, but many who had been involved in elearning in the early years criticized its uniformity—every course was now the same, and part of the experimentation with technology and associated pedagogy had been lost, as we saw in the section "Rewilding Ed Tech."

In this section, I look at some of the metaphors that we apply to VLEs. The first ones can be found in the very terms that we use to refer to them. A learning management system has implications of control and expands existing terminology, such as "content management system." Learning and by extension learners are managed in this system like resources or content. The term "virtual learning environment" possibly has a more expansive connotation, an environment being something that people can explore and in which they can spend time. Given that most of the commercial LMSs derive from North America, where that term dominates, perhaps this language has shaped the development of the technology. Table 1 provides some views of knowledge and instruction, and it can be argued that LMS maps onto the view of knowledge as "a quantity or packet of content waiting to be transmitted," whereas VLE represents the belief that "a person's meanings are constructed by interaction with one's environment." If so, then the terminology might have gone some way toward shaping the development of the tools.

A common way to think of VLEs is as tools in a toolbox. This metaphor brings to mind a tradesperson, such as a carpenter or plumber, selecting the appropriate tool for the task from the familiar toolbox. Although this is a potentially useful framing, it suggests that the educator has a similar level of expertise regarding elearning tools, but in fact many educators will not have used those outside the VLE. It is as if the tradesperson were gifted a toolbox on her 18th birthday and never upgraded it. An actual toolbox is something that the individual adds to based upon experience and preference—the contents of one person's toolbox are unlikely to be the same as another's, but everyone's VLE is the same.

In essence, people tend to find VLEs rather dull. This is partly because they are made to meet a standard need—in this they are like that other oft-criticized but widely used tool in education, PowerPoint. But what the VLE and PowerPoint have in common is that they were in the first wave of digital democratization tools. Such tools cannot be too far removed from traditional practice, or people simply will not adopt them. So, they provide a useful stepping stone toward a more digitally enhanced future. The issue with both is that for many they represent not a potential stage on a journey but the endpoint. Their ease of use and similarity to existing practice are seductive in this sense; they do not suggest or require much change in existing educational practice.

Thus, we have boring courses in VLEs and boring, bullet-pointed presentations in PowerPoint. There is nothing intrinsic in the tools that means boring is the only possible outcome—good presenters will have excellent PowerPoint presentations, and good teachers will have excellent VLE courses. Yet there is something about their proximity to standard practice that means the end result is all too often uninspiring.

Some proponents of VLEs will suggest that one version is superior, but in reality the differences among VLEs are small. Moodle, for example, is often described as a constructivist VLE, and Canvas has proponents because of its easy use. They are not all the same, but there is a tendency to overemphasize their differences. The point of a VLE is to provide a uniform collection of tools. This similarity is more significant than any difference.

The impact of VLEs is largely the same, whichever version is adopted. The problem with VLEs, like PowerPoint, lies not with the technology itself but with how institutions adopt such technology. VLEs are a considerable investment in terms of licences, resources, and time. Often they cannot be changed in and out given this investment. So, what happens is that institutions develop administrative structures and processes couched in terms of the specific technology. All of these processes can be viewed as sediment building up around an object, like something dropped in the mud. As more sediment accumulates around it over the years, it becomes harder to dislodge.

In this section, I have proposed three metaphors associated with VLEs: a toolbox, PowerPoint, and sediment. As with MOOCs, VLEs are a technology that has seen considerable application of metaphors to aid their implementation, uptake, and debate. Because of this prominent position in the ed tech landscape, VLEs and their associated metaphors are an interesting case study of how we think about education itself. In Table 1, see below, Wilson (1995) proposed that underlying metaphors for knowledge would shape how we viewed instruction.

Table 1. How Different Assumptions About Knowledge can Influence our Views of Instruction

If you think of knowledge as . . .	Then you may tend to think of instruction as . . .
a quantity or packet of content waiting to be transmitted	a product to be delivered by a vehicle
a cognitive state as reflected in a person's schemas and procedural skills	set of instructional strategies aimed at changing an individual's schemas
a person's meanings constructed by interaction with one's environment	a learner drawing on tools and resources within a rich environment
enculturation or adoption of a group's ways of seeing and acting	participation in a community's everyday activities

This underlying view will then shape the metaphor that you apply to a VLE. Farrelly et al. (2020) reviewed the different metaphors associated with VLEs in publications such as journal articles and blog posts. They proposed the following six categories of VLE metaphor.

- Straitjacket: in this metaphor, the VLE is seen as constraining the educator, for instance by reference to silos.

- Behemoth: this category suggests that constraints arise from the nature of the VLE "industry" and associated processes, so the sediment metaphor above would be an example.

- Digital carpark: in this concept, the VLE is characterized largely as a repository or content dump rather than a place of potential learning and interaction.

- Safe space: this category covers a range of metaphors high-lighting the way that VLEs provide a supportive environment, such as "security blanket."

- Smorgasbord: this category suggests that VLEs offer a wide variety of choices in terms of functionality. The toolbox might be an example of such a metaphor.

- Pathfinder: in this concept, VLEs act as pioneers for further technology and practices, an example being Trojan horse metaphors.

Even if the labels used here are not ones that you identify with, they indicate that how people talk about VLEs is nearly always couched in a metaphor. That metaphor is used either to express a viewpoint about VLEs (often critical) or as a means of thinking about how to implement them. Either way, the chosen metaphor, and perhaps more significantly its resonance with others, will influence how the technology is perceived. The VLE is arguably the central ed tech of the digital era, and similarly how metaphors are used to explain it represents the most cogent example of metaphors in ed tech.

CHAPTER 5

Ed Tech Criticism

In the previous chapter, we saw how metaphors could be used to shape criticism of a particular technology, the VLE for instance, by considering it as an artifact around which sediment accrues. In the earlier chapter on the lure of ed tech, I proposed some reasons why ed tech is such an attractive area for investment to so many venture capitalists. In this chapter, I combine these elements to consider critically some of the metaphors that ed tech vendors and media use to frame the conversation on technology, education, and change. Three prominent metaphors in this category are digital natives, Uber for education, and education is broken. The metaphor of digital natives suggested that young people had a natural affinity for technology. It was attractive in the early stages of the digital revolution, but it did not bear up to any serious analysis. Nevertheless, it has been remarkably persistent, and different forms of it arise at certain times and in various contexts. The existence of digital natives is often stated as fact in order to move on to a desirable conclusion. Another statement frequently given as incontrovertible is that education is broken and therefore in need of some urgent reform. Both metaphors establish a context within which a proposed solution then seems to be desirable. This type of solution is often couched in terms of taking a "successful" technology or business from one domain and applying it to education. I put quotation marks around successful because on closer analysis those businesses are rarely as sustainable or desirable as their proponents suggest. Uber for education is the latest incarnation of these models, but previously it has been Facebook, iTunes, Flickr, MP3, or any other new technology that gains media attention. The simplistic mapping of an approach from one sector onto higher education usually misses many of the significant differences, and models that follow the approach invariably fail, but like digital natives the "latest technology business" for education metaphor persists stubbornly.

Before I address these three prevailing metaphors, I propose the metaphor of the ed tech rapture, which seems to underpin much of the desire and narrative of the subsequent metaphors. In this initial metaphor, ed tech is presented as the means to salvation from some oncoming educational apocalypse. Interestingly, though, for all of the apocalyptic language that abounds in much of the ed tech world, most did not predict or propose ed tech's role in the pandemic. Partly, this is because it was the wrong type of apocalypse—what the COVID-19 online pivot revealed was not that radical solutions are required but that common technologies, such as the VLE, need to be deployed more widely and that the adoption, and adaptation, of existing practices are the best approach. The best thing that institutions can do for students, staff, and researchers is to try to keep things as quotidian and calm as possible. This need not mean continuing face-to-face lectures online, but it does mean that the pandemic is not the time to deploy radical pedagogies or new technologies.

Institutions should recognize, of course, the stresses created by the pandemic and not expect things to carry on as normal. Working or studying from home, being ill, or enduring the general psychological stress of living in what seems to resemble a dystopian movie mean that people are definitely not going to be as productive as normal. But this emphasis on the everyday is manifest in the focus on mundane elements that helped people to retain some sense of normalcy. Payroll is an obvious example, ensuring that the system is working if everything else goes down, similarly with websites and access to main systems. These boring, everyday things are what we take for granted, but they have been key to living through the pandemic. When you live in extraordinary times, the ordinary becomes remarkable. The same applies to much of ed tech; the large-scale deployment of online or blended learning is radical enough for many students, but it does not require new solutions. But "everyday," "mundane," and "care" are not terms that align with much of the rhetoric on ed tech.

The Ed Tech Rapture

Singler (2017) highlighted how much of the language of those who promote artificial intelligence has religious connotations: "There are AI 'oracles' and technology 'evangelists' of a future that's yet to come, plus plenty of loose talk about angels, gods and the apocalypse." Watters (2013b) also wrote about myth and faith in Silicon Valley, particularly with regard to the theory of disruption, which has a religious tone: "The structure to this sort of narrative is certainly a well-known and oft-told one in folklore—in tales of both a religious and secular sort. Doom. Suffering. Change. Then paradise." Christensen's (1997) disruption theory demands the end of one industry, which is replaced by another, and this can be viewed as an exodus to a new promised land led by a technology visionary. People often self-identify or are labelled by others as "evangelists" for a particular technology. And though this might be partly self-mocking, it aligns with the rapture view of ed tech. According to the *Oxford English Dictionary* (2021), an evangelist, after all, is someone described as "a zealous advocate of a cause or promulgator of a doctrine" or "one who evangelizes or brings the gospel to (a heathen nation, etc.)." Those who do not share the vision of the particular technology are the "heathens" in this view. There is little room for doubt or nuance in an evangelist's perspective. Visions of ed tech futures are often pitched with resonances to religious beliefs about cataclysm and salvation.

The apocalypse is a recurring theme across many religions. The *Encyclopaedia Britannica* (2006) states that "arising in Zoroastrianism, an Iranian religion founded by the 6th-century-BC prophet Zoroaster, apocalypticism was developed more fully in Judaic, Christian, and Islamic eschatological speculation and movements." A related concept is that of eschatology, concerned with the end of history and the judgment of humanity. Although versions occur in most of the main religions, apocalypticism also features in many mythologies, such as the Norse Ragnorak. Often allied with eschatology is an essential offer of salvation for believers. The Christian rapture in which Christ returns to the Earth at the apocalypse and takes his believers with him is one example, particularly prevalent in the United States. But it can also be seen in popular culture, with films such as *Avengers Endgame* and *Armageddon* and novels such as *The Hunger Games*. With extreme climate change and nuclear war distinct possibilities, a realistic form of apocalypse hangs over much of the modern era. Netflix has invested heavily in series and films set in a post-apocalyptic world (Stone, 2017), suggesting that the company knows what its viewers want. The popularity and universality across different religions, mythologies, and media indicate that apocalypse and survival are ideas that appeal in some deep sense to the human psyche. It is perhaps not hard to see why—most people share the need to belong (identity theory suggests that we define who we are by the groups that we associate with) and the desire to feel exceptional. And what stronger sense of belonging and exceptionality is there than to be one of the saved come the end of the world? That is a powerful offer. Whether that salvation comes from the pursuance of a good life determined by religious beliefs or by being well prepared with a nuclear bunker is irrelevant in some sense—the psychological appeal derives from being exceptional.

The language and concepts of the apocalypse are thus deeply rooted in the modern world, particularly in a North American context. And this apocalyptic vein is often present in ed tech futurist visions. The basic premise is that some cataclysmic change is coming that will be catastrophic for the current model of education. Here are some examples for education:

- AI will make teachers redundant: Kai-Fu Lee, a former president of Google China, says that in education he would like to "make everything go away and start from scratch" (quoted in Corcoran, 2018). He proposes a teacher-student ratio of 1:1,000. Seldon and Abidoye (2018) talk of a fourth education revolution dominated by artificial intelligence.

- Robots will transform all jobs: related to the above, automation is set to take over a lot of jobs, and higher education
needs to respond to the resultant society and economy (e.g.,
Ford, 2015).

- Universities will cease to exist: MOOC founder Sebastian
Thrun (Leckart, 2012) famously predicted that by 2062 there
will be only 10 global education providers, and his hope
that his MOOC company Udacity will be one of them can
be interpreted in eschatological terms, the end of days for
universities. Similarly, Rigg (2014) asked "can universities
survive the digital age?" as if it is an external extinction event
rather than something that universities themselves have
shaped considerably.

- Everyone will become an autodidact: Facebook's Mark Zuckerberg has a vision of "a billion students across the world . . .
able to learn on their own" (quoted in Wang, 2017). Mitra (2005)
talked of self-organized learning, with his hole-in-the-wall
project, in which children spontaneously learned using a
computer; however, when others tried to replicate his experiments, they did not find the same results (e.g., Arora, 2010).

This is not to suggest that these claims are without some element
of truth—automation will undoubtedly have impacts on jobs and the
economy, and education will need to respond to that social change.
Such claims form the context within which ed tech operates. Much
of the language of ed tech futurists is couched in catastrophic terms:
"revolution," "tsunami," "disruption," "fundamental change," "irrevoc-
able damage." It also transpires that many Silicon Valley billionaires
are investing in "some level of 'apocalypse insurance,' like an under-
ground bunker" (Robinson, 2017). So, the apocalypse, it seems, is never
far from their minds.

So, given some form of impending catastrophe, the rapture-type
offer becomes crucial. By becoming a believer—in a start-up, a particular
technology, a concept, a new labour force model, the AI singularity—you
(and your institution) can be saved. But it is always a time-limited offer,

since any delay is seen as fatal, and belief has to be total. When Thrun made his rash prediction about a limited number of global education providers, the unstated message was that, if others wished to survive, they should join him. Prensky (2016, p. 7), who invented the flawed metaphor of digital natives, says in his book that he is setting out an educational vision of "how the fragmented elements of a future vision are now coming together, allowing people who want fundamental change to finally say, 'I don't choose the educational vision of the past (and today); I choose the educational vision of tomorrow.'" What he means here is largely the acceptance of *his* vision of the future.

One can contrast this ed tech rapture with a more pragmatic approach. For example, the Open Science Laboratory at the Open University brings together a number of different online lab tools, such as a virtual microscope, virtual field trips, and live lab demonstrations with interactive elements. All of these tools—developed based upon research and feedback—benefit distance education students. This type of ed tech is not pitched as the end of education as we know it. It is focused on students' needs and in use now without reference to an imagined future. Similarly, much of the work on open textbooks is focused on direct benefits to students. These books, openly licensed so that they can be adapted, and the digital versions are free. I will show later how they can facilitate open approaches in pedagogy, but much of the language and research on them is based upon pragmatic benefits. For example, Jhangiani and Jhangiani (2017) conclude a study of open textbook adoption in Canada by stating that "students assigned open textbooks perceive these resources to be of generally high quality and value [because of] the cost savings, immediate access, portability, and other benefits they confer." Similarly, Hilton (2016, p. 573) compared open textbook adoptions and concluded that "results across multiple studies indicate that students generally achieve the same learning outcomes when OERs (Open Educational Resources) are utilized and simultaneously save significant amounts of money." These are not claims couched in a mythical future that require revolution to be realized but identifiable and realistic benefits for learners. They are, in short, *useful*.

This is perhaps a meaningful distinction to make when encountering media for ed tech. If you are uncomfortable reading an article and detect grandiose claims or a desire for fundamental change across the global education sector, it is worth asking if you are being given a "rapture" pitch or a "useful" pitch. Ironically, COVID-19, an actual crisis with connotations of an apocalypse, has revealed that it is the useful framing that we need most.

Education Is Broken

Related to the type of language seen with the ed tech rapture, a common phrase that one encounters is that in some way "education is broken." This might not seem like an analogy in the more complex mapping form, but it is a type of metaphor. Education is cast as an entity that can be broken, and this brings with it a number of connotations. First, there is a finality about the term. Consider other terms that could be used, themselves all metaphorical—one could describe education as "evolving," "adapting," "growing," "ailing," "besieged," "sustaining," or "struggling." The term "broken" implies that it is not undergoing a process but has reached a final stage. Second, use of that term suggests that something broken can be fixed. However, this is no minor repair; it is usually cast as a major overhaul by an external agent. And third, it implies judgment. With the exception of glass ceilings and piñatas, there are few things that we prefer when they are broken.

Here are some examples of the education is broken metaphor.

- Sal Khan, founder of the Khan Academy, speaking of the current model of education, stated that "the real problem is that the process is broken" (quoted in Adams, 2013).

- Campbell Brown, a former CNN host, said of her involvement with an educational website that her conversations with others "have a common starting point that the system is broken" (quoted in Daspin, 2015).

- Vermeulen (2019) began an article by stating bluntly that "education is broken. But I still believe it matters."

- Max Ventilla, the founder of an educational start-up, AltSchool, which aimed to fix education (and recently closed its schools and pivoted to become Altitude Learning), realized that he could change education because "this thing that I want personally actually calls out for the kind of solution, like a platform solution, a systemic solution, a network solution, that I kind of know how to build" (quoted in Batelle, 2016).

- Sebastian Thrun declared that "education is broken. Face it. It is so broken at so many ends, it requires a little bit of Silicon Valley magic" (quoted in Wolfson, 2013).

- An influential report from the Institute for Public Policy Research entitled "An Avalanche Is Coming" claimed that "the models of higher education that marched triumphantly across the globe in the second half of the 20th century are broken" (Barber et al., 2013).

This is not to argue that many of the criticisms that people make are not valid or that their solutions have no credit. But the aim here is to explore how the metaphorical language and framing shape the discourse. There are three problems associated with the education is broken metaphor, I would argue.

1. It is simplistic: saying that something is broken avoids having to do any subtle investigation and does not permit further analysis. Similarly, technology advocates are prone to declare that something is "dead" when in fact technologies rarely die; rather, they lose their monopolies and become specialized, adapted, mutated. One can think of radio or books in this respect and how they have changed with the arrival of the networked world.

2. It frames technological change as a crisis and not an opportunity. Once a broken metaphor is adopted, a whole set of language accompanies it and frames it as a problem

to be fixed. This is in contrast to language framed in terms of opportunity, in which some improvements move forward, whereas other initiatives do not.

3. It is used for gain: those who propose that education is broken usually have something to gain from the acceptance of this idea. Either they want to sell a solution that will mend it (after all, something broken needs to be fixed), or they want to gain prestige by being seen as someone who can at least see the means of fixing it.

If one adopts the broken metaphor, then there is the implication that one wants to start afresh, which is rarely beneficial. Instead, one might want to instigate change in a sector of higher education, for example by taking an existing course and adding some new approaches to it, campaigning for open access to all historical archives, exploring new forms of assessment, finding ways of making courses and their associated pedagogies more accessible and open, and so on. These are opportunities to build upon an approach that already does many things well. Such an approach does not dismiss the roles of those in the sector who understand it and have worked hard to realize outcomes for students. This suggests another reservation regarding the broken metaphor: it is fundamentally elitist. The underlying message is that those already in the sector do not understand technology or care about students. They are seen as being embedded in an old-fashioned way of thinking that is hopelessly broken, and this is the underlying tone of many who propose solutions to fix education. For instance, *Forbes* published a "30 under 30" list of significant people in education for 2020, and not one of them was a college or university educator; they were all founders or entrepreneurs of start-up companies (Howard et al., 2020). The implication is clear: only those outside traditional education can effect change.

Many of education's problems are not of its making; they arise from wider social issues, such as how higher education is funded, how a sector behaves when it is forced to operate in a market, how economic and social contexts for graduates are changing, and so on. There is no easy solution to any of the issues facing higher education, and I would advocate suspicion of any simple solution proposed for the varied and messy domain of education. But many of those involved in education are working on specific problems with specific approaches. Education as a whole is not a problem waiting to be fixed but a set of issues, problems, and opportunities to be addressed.

Digital Natives

There is a horror film called *The Human Centipede* (if you have previously not heard of it, I apologize for bringing it to your attention). I have no desire to see the film, but the mere idea that it contains has given me disturbed nights. In some respects, the director deserves credit for this—he has conceived the idea of a human centipede and then put it into a film, which you do not even need to see to give you nightmares. This demonstrates that bad ideas have their own power. Which brings me to the concept of digital natives. I include it in this book as a counterexample of the benefit of metaphors in ed tech. It is a powerful metaphor that did much to shape thinking about ed tech, even though it is almost entirely without basis.

The idea was proposed by Prensky (2001). He claimed in his article that "our students have changed radically. Today's students are no longer the people our educational system was designed to teach." The metaphor that he applied was that of natives and immigrants. The students who have grown up in a digital world are "native speakers of the digital language of computers, video games and the Internet." They stand in contrast to "those of us who were not born into the digital world but have, at some later point in our lives, become fascinated by and adopted many or most aspects of the new technology;[we] are, and always will be compared to them, Digital Immigrants." Such people retain "accents" of their pasts.

This was a popular view with the arrival of the internet, and Prensky was not alone in promoting the "otherness" of young people. Oblinger and Oblinger (2005) claimed as one of the defining characteristics of the net generation that "they want parameters, rules, priorities, and procedures. . . . [T]hey think of the world as scheduled and someone must have the agenda. As a result, they like to know what it will take to achieve a goal. Their preference is for structure rather than ambiguity." This prompted a question about whether previous generations exhibited a preference *for* ambiguity and lack of structure. Similarly, Tapscott (1998, p. 11), referring to education, declared that "there is growing appreciation that the old approach is ill-suited to the intellectual, social, motivational, and emotional needs of the new generation."

Bennett et al. (2008), among others, performed a thorough job of dismissing the claims associated with digital natives. They assessed the evidence in the following areas.

- Information technology use and skills among young people: although there was evidence that many young people were adept at using technology, it was not uniform and often not advanced. They concluded that "there is as much variation within the digital native generation as between the generations" (p. 779).

- Distinctive digital native learning styles and preferences: multitasking might not be beneficial, and there was evidence that the type of interaction in video games did not transfer to learning. In addition, learning style itself is a metaphor almost as harmful as that of digital natives (Willingham et al., 2015), so any call to it in validating a theory is suspect.

- Fundamental changes in education: there was little evidence of the disaffection among students claimed by commentators and doubt about whether many of the skills often proclaimed (e.g., looking up cheat codes) led to deeper learning.

Jones and Shao (2011, p. 1) reported similar findings: "Students do not naturally make extensive use of many of the most discussed new technologies such as Blogs, Wikis and 3D Virtual Worlds." They concluded that "advice derived from generational arguments should not be used by government and government agencies to promote changes in university structure designed to accommodate a Net Generation of Digital Natives."

Prensky (2011) later claimed that the metaphor of digital natives was intended only as such and that people took it too literally, although he built a considerable career upon it, so maybe he did little to dampen that enthusiasm. He is undoubtedly correct, though, that it is a metaphor, and as such it demonstrates the problem of approaching metaphors with insufficient caution or that some are just plain wrong. It was an appealing metaphor, particularly when we were in the first grip of the digital revolution and so much seemed to be different. As with Mitra's hole in the wall (2005), it appealed to a sense of the magic of technology. It seemed that one only had to give every child an iPad, then get out of the way, and educational problems would be solved.

It would be an interesting exercise to calculate how much money has been spent on the idea of digital natives over the years. There have been innumerable keynotes from people proclaiming to be experts in the area; schools, universities, and companies have hired consultants to advise them on how to deal with this strange new breed; there are extensive publications on the subject; funders have paid for research projects examining whether it has existed or not; and last, and by no means least, there are all those essays, theses, and dissertations that take it almost as a given fact. A mini-industry developed centred on a fashionable idea that under examination had no real basis in evidence.

It is a shame because the overapplication of the idea has led to a distinct reaction against any suspicion of it. There might well be some subtle attitudinal differences between people who have never known a pre-digital age; however, as Helsper and Eynon (2010) report from an analysis of technology use, age was not the only factor, and how technology was used was also influenced by factors such as location, socio-economic status, gender, type of technology, and context. The generational obsession has continued with the media focus on millennials, who have been blamed for killing everything from napkins to marriage (Donvito, 2021). The more interesting aspect is how technology made society different for everyone rather than an age-based split. Highlighting changes in the education system made possible by this new technological context were positive but wrapping them up as a generational shift has ultimately simplified the argument.

Part of the problem was that people did not consciously frame digital natives as a metaphor. Perhaps it was the sort of playful metaphor that one would put in a blog post, while acknowledging that it was not rooted in evidence and intended only as a way of thinking about current changes, but this caution was not applied to it. As a metaphor, it carries a number of connotations.

- The difference between natives and immigrants is insurmountable (this also reinforces many racist ideas about real "natives" and "immigrants").

- Being a native is superior.

- Technology use is natural and does not require any structure.

- Technology use leads to different modes of thinking and preferences in education.

- Education is fundamentally shaped by technology.

These are all considerable assumptions to make, and had it been more explicitly framed as a metaphor more people might have questioned these elements. Instead, it became accepted as a fact. Even now, when it has been widely dismissed, we see varieties of it popping up in rhetoric about the use of technology, like playing a game of bad concept whack-a-mole. Let digital natives then stand as a warning about the power of bad metaphors.

Uber for Education

There is a strange tendency in writing about technology to take any successful business and view it as an acid that burns through everything. It seems to be the most accessible metaphor, for much of ed tech is another technology company, and this is seen particularly when applying new models to education. We have had Netflix for education (Anderson, 2019), the AirBnB of education (Smooke, 2018), and inevitably Uber for education. This is in addition to the more literal instances of companies such as Amazon, Facebook, and Google and their specific educational programs.

So, although in this section I focus on Uber, it can stand for any of the metaphors that take a current technological success story and apply it to education. Kundukulam (2017) argues that Uber models are proliferating across many sectors, for example dog walking, furniture removals, even private jets. Therefore, it could be applicable to education, he asserts, suggesting that Uber's essential offering is as follows.

- Two-sided platform that matches latent supply with unmet demand: teaching can be done by anyone with certain expertise and on a wider range of subjects than the current curriculum.

- On-demand, mobile access: this is what you want when you want it.

- High-quality, community-rated suppliers: the rating of teachers allows poor ones to be filtered out.

There was the inevitable start-up (InstaEDU) that aimed to offer on-demand tutorial support "just like calling an Uber"; students are "in control of when and how they get the support they need and are assured of the high quality of the service" (Rogers, 2014).

Similarly, Burke (2015) reports an epiphany while getting an Uber and concludes that, "in response to Uber, wise government officials like those in Portsmouth, New Hampshire are eliminating outdated regulations like taxi medallions and price controls. If we want to see more innovative educational options that benefit both consumers and providers, such as teacher-led schools, then we must also liberate learning."

Burke's argument is one of unbundling education into distinct components. Unbundling education refers to "the process of disaggregating educational provision into its component parts, very often with external actors" (Czerniewicz, 2018). A learner can get content, one-to-one tuition, assessment, and recognition from different providers. The idea has occurred often in higher education since the arrival of the internet. Reporting on the Unbundled University project, which examined the extent to which it is occurring, Czerniewicz found different forms of both unbundling and rebundling taking place within and outside the university. She posed the following questions that we should ask about unbundling approaches: "Who's doing this monetizing? Why? For what purpose? Which types of knowledge are being valued? What is considered 'valuable' in higher education? What is the meaning of the academic 'brand'? Who is regulating and shaping those markets? And why is this all so urgent now?"

Woolf University, which sought to combine several of the models, has been hailed as the "world's first blockchain university," describing itself as "Uber for students, AirBnB for Professors" (Davies, 2018). The announcement of the start-up led to excited headlines such as "The University Is Dead, Long Live the University" (Hamilton, 2019). However, by 2019, the university had quietly dropped the blockchain tag (Gerard, 2019). Then it seemed to become rather quiet, and at the time of writing in 2021 its website seemed to offer courses from its own Ambrose College and a couple of other institutions. Courses cost about $1,500 each and offered personalized tuition with weekly video calls from a tutor (attempting to replicate the Oxbridge seminar model). There were no student testimonials, and Woolf University had not tweeted anything since October 2020, indicating that this model had gone the way of so many others. Transforming start-ups into viable businesses is a notoriously difficult task, of course, so the failure of some of them should be no surprise. However, maybe these ones have failed to have the impact anticipated by some because Uber for education is a fundamentally flawed idea.

One issue with such metaphors is that their proposers are uncritical of the original models. If you are suggesting a radical new model for education, then you don't want to consider all of the problems inherent in it, since it is meant to be a solution to the problems of education and should not have its own set of problems. Of course, there were considerable issues with Uber in its original form. When it filed paperwork for an initial public offering, it revealed a number of problems with Uber's business and operating models (Wong, 2019). These problems included criticisms of aggressive workplace culture, legal disputes, and poor treatment of drivers, which makes them ineligible for benefits, minimum wage, overtime, and worker's compensation insurance. Its business model has been criticized as unsustainable since Uber loses money on every ride. McBride (2019) argued that, after losing $5 billion in one quarter, its options were to pay drivers less or to increase prices, but neither is possible because drivers are already operating at near minimum wage and Uber is in a price war with competitors. Its model seems to be to take losses until it reaches a state of monopoly and then to increase prices. Yet Uber has barriers in realizing this plan since many cities and countries are effectively banning the company; for example, London, England, initially removed its licence after it was found that drivers faked their identities (Topham, 2019).

Some of these issues might be peculiar to Uber, but in general they represent factors essential to the Uber model: removing many labour conditions and undercutting costs in an attempt to establish a global monopoly. Far more than the app, and the convenience, these are the elements that we should map across for an Uber for education model, and then it might seem to be less appealing.

The basic idea of an Uber for education metaphor is that universities will be made redundant (again, it would seem) because individual learners will go directly to a marketplace of private educators. As well as the deep problems that such a model relies on, as highlighted above, people rarely consider why a sector *is not* like Uber.

In order to do so, let's examine the key elements of the Uber offering.

- A taxi ride is a brief interaction. It helps if the consumer likes the driver, but it's generally over in 15 minutes, so the consumer does not have to worry too much about an investment in the transaction.

- A taxi ride can vary in some local variables in terms of car, environment, et cetera, but it's essentially the same product every day and anywhere in the world.

- It's something for which many people possess the equipment (a car) and the capability (driving).

- The consumer has experience in this type of transaction and knows what they want from it (to get to their destination safely and at low cost).

- Getting a taxi is largely a solitary pursuit.

- Uber utilizes mobile technology and pervasive connectivity to overcome some of the limitations of the previous model, such as waving down a cab or finding the number of a local provider.

Turning to education, then, very few of those conditions are replicated.

- It requires a long time frame (certainly longer than 15 minutes usually) to achieve the required outcome. This means considerably more investment, of both money and time, from the individual, so they need to build a more complex relationship of trust.

- It is very diverse, both by place and by discipline, so any model would be required to replicate such diversity and thus be difficult to use compared with the simplicity of Uber.

- Although there might be a large pool of people who can act as tutors, the ability to construct a curriculum or design a learning activity that can be delivered effectively online is rare. Also, whereas getting a driver's licence is fairly easy, being licensed to offer formal credit for learning is a complex and highly regulated process.

- Meno's paradox argues that, if you know what you are looking for, inquiry is unnecessary; however, if you don't know what you're looking for, then inquiry is impossible. Put simply, if you are a learner in a new discipline, then you don't know what it is that you need to know. This means that it is exceedingly difficult to bypass institutions constructed to help learners overcome this very problem.

- Learning is often a social activity undertaken collaboratively with a cohort of people with similar interests and goals.

• Education is already engaging with online learning and mobile delivery, so it is not obvious that it is solving a problem.

There are already some aspects of an Uber-type model in education. For instance, it is often difficult for an institution to compete with an individual consultant on a price for research that does not require large resources. The overhead of a university makes a bid excessive compared with that of a lone researcher working out of a home office. Similarly, the online tutoring model is already under way and will likely expand, particularly in combination with OERs and MOOCs. It will be largely in conjunction with higher education, though, and not in competition with or as a replacement of it.

Most successful start-ups are based upon the transformation of a labour model, usually to the detriment of workers, and these are the elements that we should consider in any such metaphor. Also, the appeal of apps and businesses such as Uber is their simplicity for the user. It is not impossible to address all of the reservations set out above in some Uberized fashion, but it would likely end up being a convoluted and unwieldy system that would defeat the very purpose of its existence. And that is the biggest difference between Uber and education from the consumer's perspective—getting a taxi is simple (although driving a taxi well is an expert skill), gaining an education is complex. That is why we value it highly—after all, you put letters after your name to indicate your education, not to show how many taxi rides you have taken.

Uber for education can be seen as an example of a broader metaphorical trend that involves how the language and values of start-up culture have been co-opted into education. One example is the cherished status of risk, and universities, educators, and students need to be less risk averse (e.g., Furedi, 2018). However, this deification of risk is often a proxy for justifying privilege in which someone successful believes that their status is merited because they are willing to take the risk. But risk itself is often a privilege.

Blanchflower and Oswald (1998, p. 26) investigated what successful entrepreneurs had in common, and their overwhelming conclusion was that it had nothing to do with personality or genes; rather, "it is access to start-up capital that matters." Not only do entrepreneurs not have a higher propensity for risk, but also, according to Xu and Ruef (2004, p. 331) in a controlled experiment, "nascent entrepreneurs are more risk-averse than non-entrepreneurs." However, highlighting privilege is unpopular in start-up culture, which has a belief in meritocracy. But access to capital and a comfortable background seem to be the more salient factors than any personality-related ones. Groth (2015) concludes that "there's certainly a lot of hard work that goes into building something, [but] there's also a lot of privilege involved—a factor that is often underestimated."

For those who promote the value of risk, it is not limited to taking risks with their own careers, however; it also means that they are happy to risk other people's welfare too. A senior university manager once told me that they loved risk, but that was perhaps because they were unaffected by it. They would likely go on to a well-paid job elsewhere if the risk did not pay off; crucially, not only would they be untouched by any failure of their risk, but also it would likely boost their status. They become a person willing to take risk, which has increased currency in a world where the metaphor for all institutions is the Silicon Valley start-up. Compare their likely outcome with that of an academic in their 50s who might become unemployed with little chance of re-employment as a result of the change that they sought to introduce. The risk of taking a risk is not distributed evenly.

Risk becomes a vehicle by which privilege reinforces itself—only the privileged can take risks, and then risk is rewarded beyond other attributes. This is not to say that we should all be cautious and that people or institutions should never venture to do unusual things. But it is important to ask, "who is really at risk?" and to recognize that the veneration of risk comes from assuming that the start-up culture is an appropriate metaphor for higher education. The Uber for education metaphor is one example of how this culture has permeated much of education, and shapes public discourse on it, but a review of our attitudes to risk-taking reveals that it is far more deeply entrenched than simply one or two analogies of popular tech companies.

CHAPTER 6

Open Practice

In the previous chapter, I examined how metaphors are used to shape and control the narrative on educational technology and why an awareness of their use can act as an antidote to much of the rhetoric on any new technology. In this chapter, I return to the more generative metaphor approach of proposing a particular metaphor to aid our thinking and discussion on a new aspect of ed tech. My focus is not on particular technologies but on some of the practices that they have facilitated. Three of them consider what is termed "digital scholarship." The Wikipedia (2016) definition of digital scholarship is "the use of digital evidence, methods of inquiry, research, publication and preservation to achieve scholarly and research goals," and as noted in the introduction I defined digital scholarship as a shorthand for the intersection of three technology-related developments: namely, digital content, networked distribution, and open practices (Weller, 2011). It is the intersection of these three elements that is significant. After all, using Word to create an article and submit it to a journal is digital, but it is not particularly transformative. However, using Word to create an article published in an open access journal online for all to access, and then writing complementary blog posts on it, do begin to demonstrate how traditional academic practice is altered in a meaningful manner.

Understanding the complex impact of new technology on academic practice makes us reflect on our current practice and how much of it was determined by the physical aspects of a pre-digital age; for example, bringing students to a single physical location to learn from experts was the only model previously. The lecture and the university itself, then, are partly products of the limitations of a physical world. New technology removes some of these limitations but brings its own issues. In addition, the forms that arose based upon physical resources are now so entrenched that we see them not as solutions to the problem of scarcity but as the only way to realize the aims. Education is working through understanding what we want to retain from such practices and what can be altered when and for whom. Metaphors are ideally suited to help in this process.

The metaphors for digital scholarship here use Cellini's statue of Perseus that I mentioned in the introduction to assess how new technology can perpetuate old values; the concept of liminal spaces to consider the relationship between digital scholarship and convention-ally rewarded practice; and the 14th-century Czech priest Jan Hus and his views on priesthood to examine the control of research agendas.

Two other sections in the chapter focus on aspects of open educa-tional practice (OEP), which Cronin (2017, p. 18) defines as "collaborative practices that include the creation, use, and reuse of OER, as well as pedagogical practices employing participatory technologies and social networks for interaction, peer-learning, knowledge creation, and empowerment of learners."

The first form of OEP considered here is open access publishing, in particular why educators increasingly seek routes around the pay-walls created by publishers for access to content. The second metaphor highlights that, though OEP is often empowering, we should be aware of the type of hidden, unrecognized labour that it requires, for instance in organizing regular Twitter chats to create a community. The burden of this type of labour often falls unequally to women and early career researchers but is also often unrecognized in formal systems of reward.

Cellini's Perseus and Digital Scholarship

Benvenuto Cellini's bronze statue of Perseus holding aloft the head of Medusa stands in the Piazza della Signoria in Florence. I saw it after having given a talk on digital scholarship, and thus the two topics merged into this metaphor. Like any great work of art, Cellini's Perseus can bear many different interpretations, many of them contradictory, and suggest meanings never intended. In this section, I will explore three such interpretations of Cellini's Renaissance artwork and make links to aspects of digital scholarship.

The first interpretation relates to representations of power and more explicitly misogyny. Cellini's statue of Perseus is a visceral, dynamic, challenging piece of work. But it can also be read as a blatant representation of misogyny. Coretti (2015) argues that, even at the time of its creation in 1554, the statue was intended to legitimize patriarchal power and was a response to the growing power of Medici women. Medusa has long been a symbol of male oppression of female power. As Johnston (2016) argues, Medusa is a recurring theme in representations of women and can be seen as "the original 'nasty woman'": "In Western culture, strong women have historically been imagined as threats requiring male conquest and control, and Medusa herself has long been the go-to figure for those seeking to demonize female authority."

As well, as an artistic achievement, Cellini's statue was a major technological breakthrough. According to Cellini's (1728) own account, it was a Frankenstein-like act of intense, life-giving creation. His *Vita* is one of the most influential works in shaping the concept of the romantic vision of the artist generally, and more specifically of Cellini himself, as passionate, rebellious, dangerous, and inspired—a vision that would find much resonance later with figures such as Byron but that also has echoes in the lone creator myth that permeates much of Silicon Valley and the adulation of personalities such as Steve Jobs. Perseus is cast in bronze, and this medium is significant both in how Cellini portrays himself and in how he is perceived as an artist. The casting process itself is captured in a dramatic sequence in the *Vita*. Unlike a marble sculpture or a painting, the culmination of a gradual process, the bronze casting process has a definite dénouement. In the *Vita*, this is portrayed with religious allusions to the moment of creation and Christ's resurrection. Suffering from a fever, Cellini claimed that he left the casting to his workers: "I said to them, 'By tomorrow morning I shall be dead.'" He then had a vision in his fever and was warned to save the casting: "He spoke in the sad and grievous tones of those who proclaim to doomed men that their last hour has tolled. 'O Benvenuto!' he said, 'your work is spoiled; and no power on earth can save it now.'" Cellini then rushed to the foundry and through direct action saved the casting: "When I saw I had raised the dead, in despite of all those ignorant sceptics, such vigour came back to me, that the remembrance of my fever and the fear of death passed away from me utterly." This new use of casting allowed for a more realistic, vital medium, challenging the lifeless form of marble. This offered new possibilities and artistic means of interpreting and representing the world.

To turn to ed tech, new technological developments in this field similarly have embedded within them the seeds of sexism and result in reinforcing existing power structures. For example, open source provided a new method of developing software based upon community contributions and distributed tasks and roles. However, it has a distinct problem with sexism (Cuen, 2017), and many women have left the field prematurely. This has been attributed partly to how some of these communities have been founded, with accusations of sexism against key open source figures such as Linus Torvalds (Vaughan-Nichols, 2015) and Richard Stallman (Levy, 2019). What could have been established as an environment quite different from the commercial one in fact ended up reinforcing the same social norms regarding women. We see a similar story in the gaming world and online in social media, with an Amnesty International report in 2018 finding that Twitter is a toxic environment for women: "The company's failure to meet its responsibilities regarding violence and abuse means that many women are no longer able to express themselves freely on the platform without fear of violence or abuse."

In terms of digital scholarship, then, one important lesson from this metaphor is that creation, and technological development, no matter how impressive, do not occur in a vacuum and carry assumptions and embedded social values. When we promote the use of digital scholarship, these issues need to be recognized. The experience of using Twitter, for example, is not the same for a white man as it is, say, for a woman of colour.

The second interpretation of Cellini's statue is to view Medusa more straightforwardly as a monster of our own making. When we look into its eyes, we are made inhuman. This is an obvious metaphor for the dark side of the internet. We created this platform, but for all of its potential and positive elements we have also unleashed the monster of trolling, misinformation, the alt-right, bots, and interference in democratic processes. Although a considerable amount of responsibility lies with the platforms and the algorithms that they deploy to promote extremist views, it is also true that people write and distribute this content (mostly) and that social media have revealed the dark side of humanity. But Perseus can be seen as hope, in this sense, that the monster can be defeated by reflecting its gaze back at it. The role of education is to act as the shield of Perseus in this respect, to develop literacies, tools, and communities that use the communicative power of the internet as the means to take power away from the trolls.

The third interpretation in relation to digital scholarship regards the famous blood of Perseus, which pours viscerally from the severed head. Cole (1999) devotes an article to the discussion of the portrayal of this blood, deemed shocking at the time, the horror film of its day. The simultaneously realistic and excessive representation of blood flowing from the head and neck posit the viewer at the moment of death, the transition from the living state. The blood "reveals what life drains from the face and the limbs," as Cole (p. 218) puts it. In this, Perseus reminds us what death *really* means. This continual connection to reality, to what our actions mean and their consequences, is often lacking in much of the ed tech industry. How algorithms manifest themselves in people's everyday lives and their impacts on society are often greeted with a shrug. Needed is a constant reminder, like Cellini's blood, running through software coding sprints and venture capitalist huddles. It is the social impact of ed tech in which we need to be grounded.

Digital scholarship presents many opportunities and challenges for educators. This metaphor relates to how new technology gives the appearance of a different set of values, like Cellini's dynamic bronze method of casting compared with marble, but it can still replicate and reinforce existing power structures. For academics, digital scholarship potentially offers a means to reinterpret or circumvent existing systems.

For example, a widespread reputation online can be gathered through contributions rather than hierarchical structures, so in theory a PhD student can have as big an influence as a tenured professor. This is certainly true in many respects, but equally true is that the new technologies can reinforce the existing hierarchies. Stewart (2016) noted that establishing an online identity increases visibility for pre-tenure academics, and the increased network and impact offer some protection in a climate of precarious academic labour. She found that, "among the junior scholars and graduate students in the study, opportunities including media appearances, plenary addresses, and even academic positions were credited to . . . online visibility." However, researchers are also increasingly identifying the negative aspects of networked scholarship. Stewart commented that "network platforms are increasingly recognized as sites of rampant misogyny, racism, and harassment." For all of their potential to democratize the online space, social networks frequently reflect and reinforce existing prestige, with higher-ranked universities having more popular Twitter accounts (Jordan, 2017a) and professors generally developing larger networks than other positions in higher education (Jordan, 2017b).

Selwyn (2015, p. 68) argues that engaging with digital impacts on education in a critical manner is a key role of educators: "The notion of a contemporary educational landscape infused with digital data raises the need for detailed inquiry and critique." This includes being self-critical and analyzing the assumptions of and the progress in movements within digital scholarship. For example, Gourlay (2015, p. 310) argues that open education, despite its ideological position of being anti-hierarchical, can in fact reinforce existing structures, perpetuating "a fantasy of an all-powerful, panoptic institutional apparatus."

As with Cellini's Perseus, there is a paradox within digital scholarship, a new technology that allows for a different type of creation but simultaneously represents and reinforces existing structures. Recognizing that the technology alone will not address these issues and ensuring that their possible advantages are realizable for all is a duty for those who engage with them.

The Rebecca Riots and Open Access Publishing

To consider recent developments in open access publishing, particularly Sci-Hub and #ICanHazPDF, I will use the rather obscure metaphor of rural riots in 19th-century Wales. Sci-Hub, taking its inspiration from file-sharing sites for movies such as Pirate Bay, aims to provide free access to academic publications, bypassing publisher paywalls and copyright restrictions. It was founded by Alexandra Elbakyan in 2011, a student in Kazakhstan frustrated by the lack of access to scientific publications. As Bohannon (2016) reports, it is not just people in poorer countries who access Sci-Hub. As library budgets are restricted and deals with publishers become more expensive, access to many journals for those in academia is restricted. For those who do not have access to a university library, conducting research can necessitate asking others to send them required PDFs. It is also often cumbersome to access different publisher databases, and Sci-Hub offers a convenient single location. #ICanHazPDF is a more distributed approach to bypassing paywalls and gaining access to papers. In this model, someone uses the #ICanHazPDF hashtag on Twitter to request a PDF of an article that they cannot access, and often an academic who has the appropriate access will send them the required file (Gardner & Gardner, 2015). Sci-Hub has faced legal challenges and accusations of criminal activity, including hacking people's accounts. But whether it is Sci-Hub, #ICanHazPDF, or some other method, they illustrate active resistance by academics to the paywalls put in place by publishers to restrict access.

Turning to the metaphor of civil unrest in 19th-century Wales, the Rebecca Riots, as they were known, were a series of protests and disturbances in southwest Wales in the period 1839–1844. The target of the protests was usually toll gates, where anyone passing by had to pay a toll to use the road. During the riots, these toll gates were demolished by large crowds during night raids. The toll gates were seen as a symbol of a wider series of grievances, but practically they also affected the lives of farmers. The leader of the rioting crowd would be dressed in women's clothes and be referred to as Rebecca, although who fulfilled this role varied depending on location. The origin of the name was biblical, from a passage in Genesis 24:60 (KJV): "And they blessed Rebekah and said unto her, Thou art our sister, be thou the mother of thousands of millions, and let thy seed possess the gate of those which hate them." Over 200 such incidents occurred during this period, causing the government to mobilize the army and extra police. They were largely ineffective in preventing the protests, however, since the movement had popular local support, and retribution was threatened against informers.

The authoritative account of the Rebecca Riots is that of Williams (1955). Although the riots can be interpreted as a straightforward protest against an increase in the number of toll gates and their respective tolls, which had a particularly damaging effect on farmers who needed to transport lime to improve soil, Williams provides a comprehensive account of the multiple causes that led to the riots. These causes included a decaying gentry system that did not represent the people, a language barrier, poor treatment by the judiciary, a lack of agricultural innovation that depleted the soil, the strong Methodist non-conformist influence, and perhaps most significantly extreme poverty. This combination of factors created the environment in which the increase in tolls proved to be a catalyst for protest.

The 1844 report of the Commission of Inquiry for South Wales, established to examine the causes of the disturbances, identified five contributing factors. In general, although there was some criticism of the rioters, the commission interpreted their actions as arising from an intolerable set of conditions.

To return to Sci-Hub, then, and other acts of rebellion against proprietary access to academic publications, there are a number of interesting parallels. Although we can criticize a specific form that this reaction takes, as with the Rebecca Riots, a number of factors have accumulated over time to make some form of rebellion almost inevitable. Of course, an academic unable to access a paper is very different from 19th-century poverty-stricken farmers, but some of the grievances are similar.

First, the riots in Wales occurred when the toll owners became excessively greedy. Until that point, farmers had paid a reasonable toll, but a toll was increasingly interpreted as an easy means of increasing profit. Some farmers had to go through three tolls within the space of 100 metres or so—if they then had to return to fetch lime for the soil, that was six tolls just to undertake their work. Similarly, in publishing, there have been increased efforts to extract large profits. The introduction of "big deals" by which publishers sell access to a bundle of journals costs European universities (ultimately funded by taxpayers) over €1 billion annually (Kelly, 2019), profit margins of up to 40% that are unknown in almost any other industry (Buranyi, 2017), and increased costs, for example when Elsevier raised its prices by 50% in 1994 (Buranyi, 2017).

Second, the toll owners were often absent, English, and uncaring—any connection between the gentry and the local population had been lost. This reflects the decaying relationship between academics and publishers, and what was once seen as mutually beneficial and supportive is now viewed as remote, highly commercialized, and predatory. This is no longer a collaborative relationship but an increasingly exploitative one. Given such conditions, it is little surprise that many academics have few qualms about sharing a PDF via Twitter.

Third, there was sufficient local support for the Rebecca Riots to flourish without reprimand. Undoubtedly, there was intimidation involved to stop people from informing, but generally the movement was successful because the local population was sympathetic to it. Fearing an uprising similar to that in Ireland, the British government of the time was most afraid of this popular support. In academic terms also, the practice of sharing articles is now seen not as something done by a rebellious or technical clique with a strong belief in the right to free information but as something widely supported by general practice.

Fourth, the farmers in Wales were responding to the changing economic climate around them. They were missing out on the benefits of the industrial revolution (e.g., transportation links bypassed them), working soil that was increasingly of poor quality and facing the imposition of a draconian new Poor Law. Although obviously very different in degree, academics on increasingly precarious work contracts, operating in an austerity-driven economy, and threatened with excessive punishment for breaching copyright are feeling similarly aggrieved and less likely to look generously on wealthy publishing corporations. As Muscatelli (2020) highlights, researchers believe that they are working in a toxic culture: "78% of researchers think that high levels of competition are creating unkind working conditions, while 57% warn of a long-hours culture." This might not relate to open access publishing specifically, but it means that researchers are already stressed and disgruntled, so their enthusiasm for protecting the large profits of publishing houses is likely to be limited.

The message here is that, when suppression failed, ultimately the authorities were forced to concede that the grievances were valid, and a more equitable arrangement was established. Tolls are pinch points in historical change, and we are witnessing this now in the digital era. It can be difficult, confrontational, and even risky, but as one witness said of the Rebecca mob that descended on a toll it is a romantic and fearful sight.

Hidden Labour and Hunter-Gatherers in Open Practice

In this section, I explore how the field of anthropology overlooked and undervalued the role of women in hunter-gatherer societies. The two methods that I explore represent a form of hidden labour not recognized or valued because of the metrics used, and in this there is some resonance with certain types of tasks performed in digital, open practice.

In 1966, an anthropology symposium examining research on hunter-gatherer societies was convened under the title "Man the Hunter." The title was revealing in that the research generally focused on the role of men in such societies and overemphasized the significance of hunting. The organizers of the symposium, Richard Lee and Irven DeVore (1968), claimed that "man" referred to all humans and "hunter" to hunting and gathering, but the role of women and activities beyond hunting were largely absent. As Sterling (2014, p. 154) notes, "though the title 'Man the Hunter' was meant to be pithy and not to focus on men and only on hunting, this title demonstrated the biases of anthropology at the time: that men's activities were the most important and illustrative of a culture, and that hunting is the most important subsistence activity of these societies." This privileging of male activities was responsible for many of the subsequent theories that tried to claim "natural" differences between the roles that men and women undertake in society. For example, Washburn and Lancaster (1968, p. 303) claimed that "the biology, psychology, and customs that separate us from the apes—all these we owe to the hunters of time past. And for those who would understand the origin and nature of human behaviour there is no choice but to try to understand 'Man the Hunter.'"

Hunting was seen as the primary source of food and the greatest value to such societies, and the dominant provision of food by men has been proposed as the basis for the nuclear family (Lovejoy, 1981). However, hunting is often not very productive, whereas foraging provides a regular, average intake, but it is not very visible. In contrast, hunting occasionally creates a very visible bonanza but with much higher variance. Perhaps the hunter's neighbours benefit from hunting success because a kill produces more than can be consumed by one family. In this respect, societies find it useful to gain favour with hunters and thus reward them. This is the show-off hypothesis—hunting is not about acquiring more calories but about gaining status. This model suggests that women, however, avoid hunting because it "provides low unpredictable payoffs" (Gurven et al., 2009, p. 55).

There was a reaction to the dominance of men and the absence of women in the "Man the Hunter" approach, which led to a counter-symposium and collection entitled "Woman the Gatherer" (Slocum, 1975). Dahlberg (1981, p. 1) also used this title for an edited collection in which she set out how the conventional view was that "the demands of the hunt shaped the characteristics that make us human," noting the claim that hunting required intelligence, upright walking, cooperation, language, and the ability to plan. Such accounts ignored or underplayed the role of women, and from the 1970s onward more detailed research began to reveal the extent and variety of women's contributions in hunter-gatherer societies. Hiatt (1970) was one of the first anthropologists to stress that gathering was a more reliable means of obtaining food. Ironically, Lee (1968, p. 30), one of the organizers of the original "Man the Hunter" symposium, also presented research that demonstrated the importance of gathering, stating that "Plant and marine resources are far more important than are game animals in the diet." In an analysis of the diet of the !Kung Bushmen of Botswana, he found that vegetable foods comprised 60%–80% and required 2–3 days, and this was largely undertaken by women. Men also took 2–3 days to hunt but produced less in that time.

Hunter-gatherer societies vary enormously, and there is no single fixed model; for example, sometimes there is no sexual division of labour, and other times there are clearly defined roles. However, this research revealed two factors that had influenced the majority of research in anthropology. The first factor was the prioritization of the contribution of the hunter to the group, and the second was that the type of artifacts examined and the investigations conducted were shaped by this view.

The type of closer analysis mentioned revealed that often the calories provided by hunting did not represent the majority of the group's intake. The "gatherer calories" (also often small animal hunting) typically provided by women accounted for up to three-quarters of the overall intake. These calories were simply not regarded as important by the male researchers because of cultural values that they had brought to their research regarding what was significant. The contribution of women simply was not measured.

The second factor was that, following some erroneous reasoning about evolutionary psychology, it was proposed that men developed certain skills in order to hunt, such as having higher intelligence and being natural inventors. But, again, this was often a result of simply failing to look for women's contributions. Their impact can be more subtle and thus harder to detect. For example, Conkey (2003) relates how the typical account of Inca politics focuses on the actions of men but that actually a key factor in Inca expansion was the increase in corn production, which allowed beer to be brewed. This was significant in political feasts, which supported Inca control and expansion. There is thus a complex relationship among gender, food, and politics. The inventions that could be attributed to women included bowls, means of food storage, digging tools, et cetera. Crucially, though, these types of inventions would often decompose, leaving no archaeological trace, whereas a sharpened spear point would remain. Zihlman (1978, p. 13) states that "a water container, for example, would have greatly increased the distance the hominids could travel on the savanna, freeing them from relying on streams and lakes for water" but that time destroys such artifacts. In this respect, the contribution of women literally became invisible in the historical record.

This is an oversimplification of the varied and complex research in anthropology, and I recommend Saini's account (2017) for a good overview of the feminist issues (including women hunters), but it serves our purpose as an analogy, I hope. These two examples provide ways of considering what constitutes labour and the methods by which it is undervalued. The first type of work—gatherer calories—is ignored because it is not deemed important. The second type—invisible artifacts—is not seen because they are ephemeral. If we take the two as metaphors, then we can think about the type of labour in digital and open practice. For example, much of the output that constitutes digital scholarship is seen through blog posts, social media, and other more temporal forms. This is akin to gatherer calories, not deemed as worthy in the educational context as, say, one highly cited paper but in fact can contribute more to the overall academic discourse in that area.

There are also a number of support communities on Twitter and other networks. For example, a weekly tweetchat session was organized around the hashtag #LTHEChat by Chrissi Nerantzi, Sue Becking-ham, and others in 2014 and is still operating now (Vasant et al., 2018). Similarly, the community that formed around the hashtag #PhDChat provides a global support network for PhD students (Ford et al., 2014), with much of the convening and organizing undertaken by women. Such communities do much of the heavy lifting for professional development in the open, digital space beyond that offered by an individual's own institution. However, like the invisible artifacts mentioned above, this labour remains largely unseen, often because those who make decisions about reward and recognition do not inhabit these spaces. It is also often the case that women do much of these two forms of labour in digital, open spaces, and in education more generally much of the emotional labour falls to women (Bellas, 1999). This category of work is also disproportionately undertaken by early career researchers, academics on precarious contracts, and many of those professionals that Whitchurch (2008) describes as occupying the Third Space, for example educational technologists. These are all categories whose contributions are undervalued and can remain unrecognized within formal structures. Bali (2015) talked about a pedagogy of care and then reinforced it in relation to COVID-19 (2020). In the pandemic, expressing care and support, particularly for vulnerable students, is a vital component of what it means to provide education, and this kind of labour is more often undertaken by women, and it is not easily recognized within formal metrics. "Care" is not a quality that surfaces in many key performance indicators.

The first step in addressing this, I suggest, is to recognize that gatherer calories–type activities in higher education and digital scholarship are valuable; the second step is to find ways to bring to the surface the invisible artifacts–type contributions so that they are seen and noted. This can be realized through more narrative forms of promotion, a wider range of outputs considered for tenure, and encouragement in journals or at conferences to publish or present papers on these topics. It can also be realized by recognizing the impacts of other forms of hidden labour; for example, during the pandemic, the number of academic articles published with women as the first authors has declined significantly (e.g., Andersen et al., 2020). One can conjecture that this has been an effect of the increased pressures of care (children not in school, elderly parents, etc.) falling unevenly on women. In response, the FemEdTech collective (2020) called on editors to take action, such as promoting gender balance by inviting authors and being flexible with deadlines.

In 2012, I proposed a number of ways in which digital scholarship could be recognized in the process of promotion and tenure.

- Recreate the existing model by adding a layer of peer review to blog-like practices or making conventional journals more open.

- Find digital equivalents for the types of evidence currently accepted in promotion cases.

- Generate guidelines that include digital scholarship and set out broad criteria for assessing the quality of scholarly activity.

- Use metrics or statistical calculations to measure impact or influence.

- Remove or lower the significance of peer-reviewed publication,

- Award "micro-credit" for activity such as a blog post that attracts a number of comments and links (though to a lesser degree than a fully peer-reviewed article).

Similar approaches can also be adopted to recognize and promote the type of hidden labour in open practices, particularly when that labour has a direct impact on an institution's effective functioning. However, open practice itself can be seen as reinforcing privilege because, as Bourg (2018) highlights, "for marginalized people especially—a very real danger of being open on today's internet is the danger of being targeted for abuse, and harassment, for rape and/or death threats, and the danger of being doxxed." This creates the danger of promoting this kind of activity and thus forcing people to take part in it who might face such threats. Singh (2015, p. 35) emphasizes that "the people calling for open are often in positions of privilege or have reaped the benefits of being open early on." Thus, any attempt to recognize and value hidden labour needs to ensure that it does not end up paradoxically creating an environment that further marginalizes some actors. I examine this type of tension in the following section.

Liminal Spaces and Digital Scholarship

There is a tension at the heart of digital scholarship that can be summarized as "digital scholarship should count, but we don't want to count it." Bowles (2019) makes the point that, if we value certain behaviours in higher education, then we should recognize them; for example, valuing ethical behaviour by institutions is encouraged by tables such as the Times Higher Education World University Rankings (Bothwell, 2018). This is based upon metrics reflecting the UN Sustainable Development Goals and measures aspects such as gender equality, climate action, and well-being. This argument has relevance for digital scholarship in what is counted and how it is measured.

As I argued in the section on hidden labour, much of the work that might constitute digital scholarship is often not valued because it is not recognized in the same way as traditional outputs such as books and articles. What digital scholarship and open educational practice concepts have in common is the use of online technology to engage in scholarly practice, which often occurs in addition to traditional scholarly practice. Costa (2016) argues that digital scholars need to adopt a "double gamers" strategy by which they slowly implement cultural changes to practice while engaging in traditional practice to remain relevant within their institutions. There are sometimes benefits of digital scholarship that have traditional recognition or consequences; for instance, Stewart (2016) identifies benefits such as "media appearances, plenary addresses, and even academic positions" that participants credited to their digital scholarship practices. However, much of the work undertaken in digital scholarship is unrecognized and unrewarded. One solution, therefore, is to recognize and count it in the way that higher education measures everything else, including the Teaching Excellence Framework, the Research Excellence Framework, an author's h-index, university rankings, and so on.

This leads to the dilemma highlighted at the start of the chapter. In a distinctly neo-liberal environment, if the types of academic labour that many digital scholars undertake are to be recognized, then such activities need to be made explicit. But it is also true that any such measurement establishes behaviours that deliberately seek to improve any metrics, which themselves create anxiety and pressure in the system. Counting and measuring such activities would also remove much of the appeal of alternative outputs for academics and constrain the freedom that they currently enjoy. For example, imagine if producing a set number of blog posts, acquiring a certain number of Twitter followers, or achieving a requisite number of views was linked explicitly to promotion or financial reward. This system would quickly become gamified and probably be even more stressful than current citation-chasing metrics related to publications. And as seems to be inevitable, any formalization of the system ultimately would benefit existing power structures and not the people whom initially it might have intended to reward.

The concept of liminality might provide a means of thinking about this tension. Liminality is concerned with transition from one state to another; for instance, Van Gennep (1960) proposed that rites of passage act as liminal processes in which the individual transitions to a new world. Building upon this work, Turner (1969, p. 95) described liminal entities "neither here nor there; they are betwixt and between the positions assigned and arrayed by law, custom, convention, and ceremonial." Liminal spaces, therefore, are those that operate "betwixt and between" defined spaces, for example stairwells, hallways, and car parks. Preston-Whyte (2004, p. 349) writes of the beach as a liminal space: "The beach is a place of strong magic, . . . a space that is neither land nor sea, a zone of uncertainty that resonates with the sound of ever-changing seas, a setting that is, by turns, calm, tranquil, and soothing or agitated, unruly, and frightening."

As such, liminal spaces and practices are often concerned with transition from one state to another. In mythology, however, liminal spaces are not necessarily valued for an individual becoming something else: that is, there is no desired end state after the transition. Instead, they are revered as spaces that operate at the thresholds of worlds—the betweenness itself is valued. For instance, in the Welsh folktale of the Mabinogion (Guest, 1848), liminal spaces are those that connect to the otherworld. In the First Branch, Pwyll sits on a mound that "whosoever sits upon it cannot go thence, without either receiving wounds or blows, or else seeing a wonder" (p. 80). He sees and meets the mythical Rhiannon, who will become his wife as a result. The mound acts as the liminal space here between worlds, and it is valued for that otherworldliness, for operating between two spaces but being distinct from both of them.

The practices of digital scholarship such as writing blogs or networking through social media can be seen as constituting a liminal space: that is, a space between formal and informal, simultaneously outside and inside the university. Oravec (2003) suggests that blogs occupy a "middle space" between face-to-face and online education. Wood (2012, p. 96) proposes blogs as a liminal space for student teachers, in which blogging "is a process leading to fundamental change in the person undergoing the initiation, as their view of the world is altered while they are given time to consider both social and personal difficulties and beliefs and to learn from 'elders' who themselves have gone through the rite of passage." Purdy and Walker (2013, p. 11) suggest that composition classes (which can be akin to blogging) allow for the construction of new identities, which help to create a liminal space that aids transition because "higher education attempts to create a boundary between itself and the 'outside world.'"

Taking these perspectives on liminal spaces, then, it is possible not to surrender digital scholarship to the machinations of rigorous measurement and still recognize that such scholarship requires real labour to be effective. To do so, we should seek to establish "liminal spaces" within our institutions and workloads. That is, there is work that can be recognized as valuable, just as the burial mound is revered in the folk tale, but this respect means that we do not seek to excavate it and examine it too closely. How this would work exactly needs careful negotiation; many universities still have some notion of "research time," so perhaps there is value in allowing digital scholarship to be recognized as a valid component of that without then imposing strict metrics to it. I concede, however, that it is not without risk, and sometimes the transitions in liminal spaces are not always welcome ones. As Waite et al. (2013, p. 61) put it, liminal spaces "may also be troublesome as personal identity shifts in an attempt to reach new understanding as old ways of doing and thinking about things are discarded." There will be some inevitable discarding through the process of digital scholarship while ensuring that what remains is useful and valid.

Hussites and Guerrilla Research

In this section, I address a particular aspect of digital scholarship: namely, the impact on the means by which research as a whole can be undertaken in a networked society in which data and resources are abundant and the means of dissemination are open. Much of what we recognize as research is determined by the scarcity of data and control over routes of dissemination such as journals. Although traditional modes of research are still, and will remain, significant, the digital era provides an opportunity both to conduct research in different ways, using new methods, and to reimagine what we consider to constitute scholarly research. For those of us grounded in academia, our view of research has been formed by the approaches to resource scarcity, so it can be difficult to conceive of different perspectives. This is where metaphor provides us with a useful tool, and the one that I use here relates to a 14th-century Czech priest to make it as distant from our target domain as possible. The story of the priest, Jan Hus, is interesting in itself, so we will commence with that and then turn to its relevance for digital scholarship and research.

Hus was born around 1372, and he later argued for reform of the Catholic Church through his public preaching and his writing. He was one of the main influences on Martin Luther and has been seen as one of the primary reformers before the Reformation. His main arguments were summarized in his 1413 tract *De ecclesia*, which proposed that the word of God should be preached freely and in common languages, that everyone (who was baptised) was a member of the church, that the rich should give their wealth to the poor, and that people should not pay for elaborate burials. Perhaps most radically, Hus "gave the laity the choice whether or not to obey priests, saying that they should acknowledge only those priests who lived holy lives" (Klassen, 1990, p. 261). This choice extended to the pope, and people could question any clergy whom they deemed not to be leading a holy life, including the accumulation of wealth. His policies "made the people sovereign" (Klassen, 1990, p. 261).

Although his teachings were popular with the poor in Bohemia, they were not well received, perhaps unsurprisingly, by the church and the pope. Hus was excommunicated by a papal bull and put into exile, and renowned Hussite scholar Fudge (2013, p. 2) states that he "had been judged unworthy of humanity and expelled from the Christian community. Should he die, he had no right to a proper religious burial; his corpse was considered fit only to be discarded. . . . Whoever might touch him, whoever dared speak to him or attempt to give him any assistance whatever ran the risk of criminal prosecution leading to a similar fate. He was cursed and without human remedy." Hus was tried at the Council of Constance, where he refused to recant his views and was convicted for heresy and burned at the stake in 1415.

After his death, his followers became known as the Hussites. They refused to recognize the pope and formed around a set of beliefs known as the Four Articles of Prague, which continued the arguments about preaching freely, anti-elitism, and anti-wealth. The Hussites would go on to be a formidable fighting force, aligned with Czech nationalism and defeating five papal crusades in the Hussite Wars. They are credited with developing an early version of the tank, the war wagon, a reinforced peasant cart with planking from which guns could be fired through slots.

It is easy, particularly in a short section, to make broad generalizations about Hus and the Hussites, portraying them as a kind of utopian force. For example, Hus was not the first to start public preaching and using a native language, rather than Latin, and it is overly simplistic to think of Hussites as a single entity, for the group was composed of many different factions with a range of views. Hus is sometimes portrayed as a proto-Marxist, and there are certainly elements of that in his calls for the redistribution of wealth. Fudge (1998, p. 25) argues that this too is an oversimplification, noting the common belief that "the Hussite Revolutionary Movement essentially comprised a social and economic struggle against the exploitation of late medieval Feudalism," but he "finds the Marxist explanation wanting." However, Klassen (1990, p. 249) argues for the legacy of Hus in modern thinking, concluding that "ideas such as religious toleration, popular sovereignty, the dignity of the common man and the destructive powers of greed and violence all raised by the Hussites have survived within European civilization." However, in the analogy that follows, it is worth bearing in mind the necessary simplifications that I have made.

In *The Battle for Open* (Weller, 2014), I proposed the idea of "guerrilla research" as an example of transformed practice that openness allows. Open practice in a digital, networked world allows us to rethink what academic research means, and this is where the link to the Hussites lies. We tend to think of research as comprising certain elements: it is often externally funded research, it produces a traditional output such as a journal article or book, it undergoes a pre-selection evaluation, and it is often in competition with other proposals. This attitude toward how research is conducted and what it looks like was shaped prior to the digital revolution, and though some of that conceptualization remains true many possibilities are opened up by new technologies and approaches. It is now possible to create your own journal, disseminate findings, interrogate open data, conduct open research, and analyze online resources all without research grants. None of these approaches should be seen as replacing traditional approaches to research. They are not superior to them but complementary.

What these new approaches have in common is that they do not require permission, except maybe in relation to time allocation. In his review of the film *The Social Network*, Creative Commons founder Larry Lessig (2010) pointed out that the removal of barriers to permission was the really significant part of the Facebook story: "What's important here is that Zuckerberg's genius could be embraced by half a billion people within six years of its first being launched, without (and here is the critical bit) asking permission of anyone. The real story is not the invention. It is the platform that makes the invention sing."

The same freedom applies to scholarly practice also, including how we conduct research, disseminate results, and teach. Unger and Warfel (2011) proposed the idea of guerrilla research in software development, and a similar lightweight approach can be adopted in academia. Guerrilla research has the following characteristics.

- It can be undertaken by one or two researchers and does not require a team.

- It relies on existing open data, information, and tools.

- It is quick to realize.

- It is often disseminated via blogs and social media.

- It doesn't require permission.

Using open data, free tools, and social media for dissemination, then, people can undertake useful, impactful research that previously would have required funding and extensive data collection. This type of research can be conducted without permission, meaning that the methods and focus of research can be broadened beyond what is formally approved and funded. For instance, in the later section on rhizomatic learning, there is an article by Bali et al. (2016) that uses an auto-ethnographic approach to analyze the open course "Rhizo14." Or, in the section on MOOCs, I referenced the completion rates analysis by Jordan (2014), which used openly reported MOOC completion rates, open access data visualization tools, and blogs to disseminate findings.

These are two examples of research conducted on the basis of open tools, data, and practice.

In *The Battle for Open* (Weller, 2014), I set out how the current research model is wasteful of time and money, but it goes unremarked on because it is accepted practice. One example is the development of research bids to funders. The majority of them are unsuccessful, yet they are often the results of months of work by a coalition of partners. In 2014, I estimated this at about 65 years of people time for the United Kingdom for just one funding agency, and competition for funding has only increased since then. This was just a "back of the envelope" figure, but it demonstrates the inherent waste of time and money in the current model. Much of the hard work in those bids is lost since they are not made openly available. This is not to suggest that the peer-review process is not valid but that the failure to capitalize on bids represents a substantial waste of resources. The point is to illustrate that, though guerrilla research might seem to be unappealing because it does not bring in external funding, in fact it might represent a more efficient use of resources by academics who have the skill, predilection, and appropriate subject area for working in this manner, but they are often forced to operate in the traditional funded model to gain recognition.

Many of these bids represent valid research but fail on technicalities related to the proposal format. A more open approach to research development would reduce the overall waste. The competitive nature of bidding often precludes the public sharing of bids, though, especially in the development stage, and as such it represents one of those areas of tension between open scholarship and traditional practice. Guerrilla research might represent a means of realizing some of the proposals, although in some areas, particularly science, it isn't possible. For example, if a proposal is to investigate the impact of COVID-19 on academic staff, then it might be based upon surveys, interviews, focus groups, a conference, and subsequent analysis. A guerrilla research approach, instead, might analyze Twitter sentiment on the hashtag #onlinepivot, review relevant blogs, examine different institutional statements, and publish the findings via a blog or self-hosted webinar. This would take considerable time to realize, which institutional policies would have to recognize, but it would not require the type of funding or legitimation of the first approach. It would produce different results, but they would be valid and of interest.

What has all this got to do with a 14th-century Czech priest? His premises were that the people did not need priests to relate to God, that everyone baptised formed part of the church, and that the papal hierarchy should be undermined. My intention here is to comment not on the theological argument but on the structures that grant permission for certain types of activity. For the Catholic Church in 14th-century Europe, one can read research councils in this analogy. They hold power and money, and they decide what is legitimate—the church in terms of what was valid holy practice, research councils in terms of what constitutes appropriate research. As in churches, there are significant rituals performed for research funding to demonstrate worthiness of benediction, but such a comparison is probably stretching the metaphor too far. More apt is the Hussite view that everyone is equally holy, and in my analogy this can be interpreted as everyone is their own research council. With more lightweight, open models of research, permission to conduct practice is not required, and dedicated buildings and structures are not always necessary either. The approval of a council is not always required to reach an audience.

My argument here is not to overthrow research councils, for they are still vital to certain types of research, but to propose that often there are low- to zero-cost alternatives available that might get at some of the research questions. They should be considered and valued by institutions as valid models of conducting research. But let's leave the last word to a quote commonly attributed to Hus: "Love the truth. Let others have their truth, and the truth will prevail."

Music Metaphors

Music as a metaphor readily springs to mind for many, yet I am reluctant to engage with many such metaphors, largely because doing so often results in the unedifying sight of middle-aged men attempting to recapture their youth or demonstrate their street cred. But two metaphors in this genre are worth exploring because they highlight some of the possibilities of digital scholarship and are good examples of how metaphors can shape thinking.

Edupunk

The first of the music metaphors is that of edupunk, which Groom proposed in a blog post in 2008, bemoaning the corporatization of elearning and its move away from more experimental foundations: "Corporations are selling us back our ideas, innovations, and visions for an exorbitant price. I want them all back, and I want them now!"

Punk was a useful and neat metaphor for encapsulating the DIY spirit that formed much of the early elearning boom. Educators could create their own courses, pull in resources from the open web, and encourage students to utilize what was available online. As *Wired* magazine indicated, "avoiding mainstream teaching tools like Powerpoint and Blackboard, edupunks bring the rebellious attitude and DIY ethos of '70s bands like the Clash to the classroom" (Keats, 2008).

The original punk movement in the United Kingdom started around 1976 and was a reaction to the corporate music industry and what was seen as the increasingly bloated and pretentious music of the prog rock scene. The ethos of punk was that anyone could start a band, and many people did. This led to a flurry of creativity in the late 1970s and into the 1980s in the music scene. This approach also led to other endeavours, including the founding of independent record labels, the development of punk fanzines, fashion, and a wave of new filmmakers.

Perhaps the key element of the punk ethos was the removal of barriers or the need for permission. This was analogous to the freedom that the web offered. The web allowed anyone to publish; the restrictions of requiring a print setup and a distribution mechanism were removed, just as the barriers to starting a band and distributing music had been challenged by the punk movement. It was this element that Groom tried to capture with the term "edupunk." It had a brief flurry of attention, making the *Wired* jargon list of 2008, as highlighted above, and Kamenetz (2010) used it to frame a book around changes in higher education. Revisiting edupunk in 2018, Groom noted that "the concept was pretty simple, take back the online spaces where teaching and learning happens from the dreary, fl[u]orescent-lighted discussion boards of the Learning Management Systems. . . . Reclaim a sense of ownership and experimentation within educational technology and explore the possibilities."

Although it generated a number of blog posts, it also smacked somewhat of middle-aged men (I myself among them) reliving their teenage years, and it is a good example of the domain metaphor being too overpowering to be effective. If you did not like punk music to start with, then the metaphor was not very appealing and perhaps even damaging to the points made. Taste in music is a very personal thing, and the implication that punk was better than other forms was no doubt off-putting for many. It also became a tool wielded by those who wished to dismantle the education system, with a "school yourself" philosophy, and edupunks in effect acted as "useful idiots" for a neo-liberal agenda, which Groom (2010) rejected, but he acknowledged that the term had morphed into various interpretations.

Like all generative metaphors that carry some weight, it was perhaps more interesting because of what else it suggested. In *From Gutenberg to Zuckerberg*, Naughton (2011) makes the point that we are living through a revolution and that it is quite difficult to see what the outcome will be. Calling the digital shift a "revolution" is itself a metaphor, but let us assume that it does represent one in many respects. Naughton suggests that revolutions promote both pre- and post-forms of thinking, and people speak of absolutes rather than the more complex reality.

This was certainly how the original punk movement portrayed itself—any music prior to 1976 was irrelevant, but as with nearly all revolutions this was not the case, and the actual picture is far more subtle and interesting. Although for many people of a certain age punk was a defining revolution in music, it was not as all-encompassing as history has painted it. Plenty of people were unmoved by it, and their musical tastes remained largely untouched. And there were others who didn't like punk but went on to become new romantics, a musical development undoubtedly influenced by the possibilities that punk had awoken in people. So it is with edupunk; many educators are completely unmoved or unaffected by it, and others might not even know of it but still make use of some of the approaches that it fostered.

Another extension of the metaphor is that punk itself became both a commercial entity and something much darker beyond its original rebellious roots. Although there was a strong anti-racist ideology in punk, it also morphed into the neo-Nazi Oi! movement of skinhead punk bands. So it is with much of the open web that edupunk idealized, for it is now a haven for far-right groups, conspiracy theorists, and misinformation. This is far removed from the original intentions and hopes that it might have fostered.

Educator as DJ

The second music metaphor to explore is that of educator as DJ. Scott Leslie talked about the open educator as DJ (Clow, 2010), suggesting that DJs could mix music when it became abundantly available, and the same was now true for knowledge. Educators had access to online resources that they could remix effectively, creating something new, as DJs do with a set of records that they sample and mix. Leslie (Clow, 2010) proposed a six-stage sequence for the educator as DJ.

- Search: just as good DJs spend a lot of their time searching for records from which they can sample beats and make selections, so too the open educator must start by finding educational resources. Developing appropriate search skills, networks, and repositories is a new ability for educators.

- Sample: having found records, the skilled DJ takes out the elements that are useful in another context or when remixed with other elements. Similarly, the educator needs to extract parts of the learning content that they wish to use or modify. Simply reproducing all of it wholesale might be appropriate sometimes, but often it requires selection. This also requires a skill set that might include knowledge about licences or technical skills associated with different formats.

- Sequence: the next step is to sequence the samples together or, for the educator, to create the course or unique learning material. This can be done using a number of tools such as wikis, blogs, or open learning platforms.

- Record: DJs might add in their own sounds or music generated from other tools, and Leslie suggests that educators will not always find what they require and so will need to create their own content to add into the sequence. This can be in any format—audio, video, text—but the emphasis will be on low skill level rather than professional production.

- Perform: the DJ is as much a performer as a singer, and the open educator is still involved in the act of teaching. This can be asynchronous or synchronous, using a variety of tools from Zoom to blogs.

- Share: for the open educator, sharing is an important part of the process, and, if open resources and tools have been used in the preceding steps, then they can make the content part of the ongoing open knowledge base.

Leslie (Clow, 2010) emphasized that these are not the only sequences, and not all steps are necessarily required, but DJs do have their own sequences. His focus here, as with edupunk, was on the nascent possibilities of the open web to change how education could be conducted. Looking back at this list, there might be some naive optimism about it, but there is also a challenge to reconsider how educators work and the skills that they require. This challenge was one that higher education in general failed to take up, but had it done so sector wide it is likely that the online pivot enforced by the pandemic would have been less traumatic.

The educator as DJ was also proposed as a metaphor by Wiley (2005), who used it to explore the need for educators to develop responsiveness to online learners. Wiley argued that learners now have alternatives that they can avail themselves of in the form of online learning resources. This is akin to nightclubbers abandoning the dance floor if the DJ misreads the audience. As Wiley asks, "how would the dynamic change if learners felt free to vote with their feet like the clubbers, to walk off the dance floor whenever a class became too lame? This is exactly what online education enables them to do, and this is exactly why paying attention to the social component of these experiences is so much more critical in online learning."

An extension of the educator as DJ metaphor was proposed by Greene (2020), expanding to the elements of hip hop as a metaphor for open education. There are four elements of hip hop culture commonly accepted (Price & Iber, 2006), with a fifth element often added. Greene suggests playfully that they map onto open education as follows.

- Lyricism (rapping): rapping is perhaps the most well known of the five elements and often confused with the whole. It was one part of the initial hip hop experience with an emcee rhyming freestyle on the mic over the music. For Greene, this is analogous to a faculty member in front of students. To reinforce Wiley's or Leslie's points, this is part of the performance and reaction of teachers. Greene states that "it's not just what they say, it's how they say it."

- Turntablism (DJing): lacking physical instruments, early hip hop pioneers made music with what they had at hand, namely records and record players. Grand Wizard Theodore is credited with the technique of scratching, whereby each record could be seen as a source of new sounds and samples. Along with other pioneers, he essentially transformed the technology of the record player from an output device to a creative instrument.

The open educator equivalents are the educational technologists and instructional designers, particularly those who explore and convert the technology into different uses, perhaps akin to the edupunk ethos (Greene, 2020).

- Breakdancing/b-boying: new forms of dancing were an important component of the early hip hop culture, known as breaking or b-boying. This kind of dancing saw people take turns, encouraged by those around them to perform new moves. Greene suggests that this willingness to share techniques and encourage each other is also seen in the network of open educators.

- Graffiti: this can be seen as the visual expression of hip hop; like the punk movement, it developed an aesthetic of its own that went far beyond its immediate culture. For Greene, this has resonance with openly licensed images, which can be reused, or tools such as the Remixer machine from Bryan Mathers.

- Knowledge: knowledge of the movement and the cultural significance of hip hop and its politics is given as the last element. Knowledge of the sector allows practitioners to build upon it more effectively.

As with the edupunk metaphor, there is the danger of the metaphor here being overpowering, but it provides a means of thinking about aspects of open education. It is noticeable that these metaphors are all concerned with the possibilities that operating in the open provide for education. Both punk and hip hop have as part of their appeal a strong DIY ethos. Whereas punk was about a sweeping away of the old regime, hip hop and DJing might provide a more apt metaphor with their foundation in creating new forms of art from existing elements.

One last metaphor of the educator as DJ is one that I proposed (Weller, 2007). This takes the radio version of the DJ rather than the nightclub, hip hop performer one. With music services such as Spotify, Amazon Music, and Apple Music, listeners can now get access to almost any music that they wish to listen to with a simple click. They can also receive personalized playlists and tailored recommendations and follow others for different music. Given this abundance, the days when you could hear new music only via a radio show are long gone. One might expect from this that there would be a decline in radio listening since one of its core value propositions has now been eroded. But that does not seem to be the case. During the COVID-19 lockdown in 2020, radio listening increased significantly (Paine, 2020). So, what makes people want to listen to broadcast radio? The answer, in part, is the DJ. People tune in to connect with the human presenter as well as to hear the music. There is an analogy here to educators and online resources. Just as Spotify provides free content, but some people like a DJ to provide context for it, so too, for example, OER provides free educational content, but the educator (or academic institution) puts it into context and provides guidance. The educator, like the DJ, provides the human aspect and the skill of connection.

Ultimately, I believe that, rather like political metaphors, music metaphors tend to overpower the intended analogies, and people pay more attention to the domain than the mapping. As with edupunk, they also have a tendency to run away with themselves. They can also end up being rather exclusive—meaningful to fans of that music or genre but off-putting to those who are not—rather than inclusive. However, I do think that from a personal perspective they offer a rich source to start exploring metaphors, and as the examples above illustrate in places they can help us to find a way into a new practice.

CHAPTER 7

The Coronavirus Online Pivot

Throughout this book, I have made occasional reference to the online pivot that occurred in the wake of the 2020 COVID-19 pandemic. Universities, colleges, and schools were all closed for face-to-face teaching to reduce the risk of infection. In May 2020, UNESCO reported that over 85% of the world's student population, some 1.4 billion learners from 188 countries, were affected by the closure of educational institutions at all levels in response to the pandemic. The only alternative for many institutions was to deliver some form of education online, and this sudden switch became known as the pivot online (or online pivot). In the immediate aftermath of the pandemic lockdown, this was often realized by conducting synchronous sessions, lectures, and classes online using a tool such as Zoom. However, this quick solution is unlikely to be sustainable in the long term, and with universities now offering a range of provisions—from fully online to blended to on-campus learning with enforced social distancing—more sophisticated and structured use of online learning will be required.

The pandemic and the subsequent online pivot have revealed many existing attitudes to online learning and considerable ignorance of existing practices. In the longer term, the pandemic will make many HEIs review the overall robustness of their offerings and seek to move portions online as a possible response to any future crisis. This has caused considerable consternation among many in senior positions in universities. Often they have spent their careers advocating the superiority of the campus experience over distance and online versions of learning and thus have a lot of personal capacity invested in this view and many construction projects based upon it. Shifting learning online, partially or wholly, is not a problem that they wish to have.

In addition, the time frames were short and the financial pressures considerable. Interest increased among external providers to solve the problem for universities. This might be effective in the short term, but in the longer term any effective solution will require staff development and establishment of new forms of support for students. This precarious relationship among universities, vendors, and learners is explored in the first of the metaphors in this chapter.

One of the biggest impacts of the pandemic on higher education is likely to be financial. The pandemic has revealed the fragility of the finances in the sector—over expenditure on campus buildings, reliance on the fees from international students, vital support staff and academics on precarious employment contracts, the impact of expensive student fees in countries such as the United Kingdom, and so on. It can be difficult to predict the long-term impacts of these issues. For example, after the banking crisis of 2008, there were many predictions about what changes would result, but the real long-term impacts were often secondary ones. The rise of populist leaders and causes such as Donald Trump and Brexit can be seen as a result of the long tail of the banking crisis, which led to austerity, which in turn caused unemployment and resentment among the white working class that could be exploited by xenophobes and nationalists. Such secondary effects are more difficult to predict, but one likely consequence in higher education is that HEIs will seek to make themselves and their models more robust to withstand any such impacts.

From an ed tech perspective, Tony Bates (2020) predicts an increase in the adoption of online learning but suggests that predictions that every institution will go online permanently are overblown. Some might switch to a predominantly online model, with a levelling out of about 25% of institutions offering fully online learning. Bates suggests that in the next five years far more, about 70%, will offer a blended or hybrid model, mixing online and face-to-face learning more effectively than now. Having made investments in ed tech, gained some of the benefits of a distributed model, and now keen to build in resilience against further crises, HEIs will offer a mixture of online and campus learning as the norm.

Jaws and the Online Pivot

Steven Spielberg's 1975 film *Jaws* is divided into two clear acts. The first act takes place on the island of Amity, gearing up for its summer boom of the 4th of July. The central character, Chief Brody, wants to close the beaches because people are being eaten by a shark, and he rightly assumes this to be undesirable. His nemesis is the town's mayor, Vaughn, who wants to keep the beaches open because of the impact that closure will have on the local economy. There are some immediate parallels here in the pandemic, with Trump in the United States and Boris Johnson in the United Kingdom initially wanting to keep businesses open. In higher ed terms, there is also a more stylistic analogy with this first act (although I will focus on the second act). In the first act, Amity Island is presented as idyllic, all bright sunshine and white picket fences. The shark lurks out there in the deep, the dark, the unknown. This might be how some in higher ed have been operating too: the pandemic (the shark in this analogy, obviously) has brought into focus many issues that have been hitherto ignored or downplayed. The reliance on income from overseas students by many universities is akin to Amity's reliance on summer dollars. There are frailties everywhere in Amity that the shark's presence exposes: minor corruption, class conflict, incompetence, distrust of outsiders, and precarious employment. You can map most of them onto higher ed also, for the weaknesses in a fragile system have been exposed.

After the body count rises, the mayor is forced to face the inevitable consequences. The first act ends with Brody hiring fisherman Quint, accompanied by shark expert Hooper, to kill the shark. Despite desires to carry on, higher ed reached a similar switch in the mood and tone of its narrative when the online pivot began. It went through the "beaches will be open on the 4th of July" phase, when officials in higher ed thought that it could carry on business as usual. This mentality reappeared among some officials when the new academic year started in September

2020, with many universities operating on campus only to shut down shortly after as cases of coronavirus soared. University campuses are a perfect environment for viruses to spread, combining communal living, multiple intersecting social networks, and people in proximity to each other (Paltiel et al., 2020). As Kernohan (2020) points out, with students travelling from all over the country, this presents a problem of viral spread beyond the campus. In *Jaws*, Hooper declares that a shark "is attracted to the exact kind of splashing and activity that occurs whenever human beings go in swimming. You cannot avoid it." This is not true, by the way, for sharks actively tend to avoid people (McKeever, 2019), but for our analogy it is akin to how coronavirus is spread by exactly the actions of campus students: it is unavoidable. Hooper suggests that there are only two ways to defeat the shark: "You either gonna kill this animal or you're gonna cut off its food supply." Until uptake of the vaccines became sufficiently widespread, the only option to control the virus was, metaphorically, to take away its food supply.

The second act of *Jaws* focuses solely on the *Orca* boat and the three main protagonists. For this part of the analogy to work, it is important to accept that *Jaws* is not really a movie about a shark. It is, in one reading, a movie about three aspects of humanity (or specifically masculinity). There are many different interpretations of the movie, such as a patriarchal myth, with men killing the symbolic female (Caputi, 2010), a critique of capitalism (Frentz & Rushing, 1993), or angst about the atomic bomb (Rubey, 1976). A further perspective is that in the movie women and people of colour are excluded, but that would require a dedicated interpretation to do it justice. As we saw in the hunter-gatherer section, marginalized groups often bear the brunt of the impact, perhaps both of the shark and of the pandemic. In fact, this variety of interpretations is the film's, or more specifically the shark's, contribution to society: "None of these readings can be said to be wrong or aberrant, but their very multiplicity suggests that the vocation of the symbol—the killer shark—lies less in any single message or meaning than in its very capacity to absorb and organize all of these quite distinct anxieties together" (Jameson, 1979, p. 142).

In the more straightforward interpretation of three aspects of masculinity, each core aspect of socialized masculinity is represented by one of the main characters: Brody is the family, domesticated man; Hooper, the intellectual man; Quint, the macho man. Bailey (2020) sums it up by saying that the "three protagonists fall on distinctive points in the masculinity continuum." A Freudian analysis might interpret them as ego, super-ego, and id, respectively. The three are in competition on the boat, and ultimately only two can emerge from their confrontation. They form a triangle, essentially, with each element in tension with the other but just maintaining a stable pact.

When the shark comes along, this fragile balance collapses. As anyone who has balanced cards to make a triangle will know, a collapsed line with two points is more stable, and it will revert to this with the slightest disruption. What has this to do with the online pivot and ed tech? In our analogy, Brody represents learners—we want to do right by them. Hooper, the intellectual, represents the academy and educators. This leaves the self-proclaimed man of reality, Quint, who represents ed tech vendors and content vendors. Prior to the arrival of the "shark," they co-exist, if uncomfortably, like the three characters, but this is fragile. With the arrival of the "shark," only two can survive ultimately. It can be any two but not all three.

We can view educators and ed tech vendors in a financially beneficial relationship that sees learners essentially as customers with wallets. Post-pandemic there will be a move to seek vendors to create online courses, and universities will do so to ensure their income streams, particularly from overseas students. HolonIQ (2021) reported a significant rise in the number of universities signing partnerships with commercial content providers in the first half of 2021, beyond expectations, which suggests that this was a reaction to the online pivot. Alternatively, after the pandemic, the lack of agility in universities and their frail finances might see some collapse, and consequently learners will turn to commercial providers. In this scenario, vendors and learners engage in a deprofessionalized, unbundled education market. The same HolonIQ report also highlighted the commercial acquisition and investment of learner platforms such as EdX, FutureLearn, and Coursera, suggesting that many commercial players now see an unbundled online learning market as a wise investment. The third scenario (and the one that plays out in *Jaws* with Hooper and Brody surviving) is that educators and learners exist in a higher education system that, after the pandemic, will be based upon education as a social and public good. The "shark" will not let all three emerge from the crisis, and now we get to decide which pair it is.

Of course, none of this is actually inevitable, and you can do your own analogy with any film that you choose, in which vendors, educators, and learners all co-exist for mutual benefit. But in this scenario, only two get to paddle back to shore. *Jaws 2* gives us the perfect tagline for 2021 also: "Just when you thought it was safe to go back to campus. . . ."

The Internet Design and Robustness of Education

The pandemic has brought into sharp focus several structural weaknesses in the higher education system. They included the proximity of many people in one centralized location, which as highlighted in the previous section created a perfect culture for a virus to spread, and when that location was closed it was difficult for many of the functions of education to continue. The reliance on the lecture as the only model of delivery meant that other options were not readily available. The use of high-stakes examinations that required many individuals to be physically co-located at a specified time allowed no room for disruption, resulting in difficulty assessing students. In summary, the function of higher education was too closely allied with its physical instantiation. Once the buildings closed, the activities associated with them had no reliable means of continuation. Through the heroic efforts of many involved in education, including educational technologists, those activities did find a way to continue via the online pivot, but this is not a sustainable model. Although the crisis came in the form of the COVID-19 virus, there are other forms that it could have taken: climate change, increasing political unrest, different pandemics, and so on. COVID-19 made it apparent that the model of higher education largely adopted across the globe was not sufficiently robust.

If we want to design a more robust system, then there are plenty of metaphors from which to choose, and we will look at the idea of ecological resilience in the next section. One such model is from a system designed from the outset to be robust: namely, the internet. Paul Baran, the architect of the original design, proposed a communication system to the military that would be robust in the event of a nuclear attack. Naughton (1999, p. 97) states that Baran used three design principles: "One, avoid centralisation like the plague—because any centralized system can be disabled by a single well aimed strike; two, build a distributed network of nodes, each connected to its neighbours; and three, build in a significant amount of redundancy in the interconnections."

Building upon Baran's decentralized model, the internet was designed to connect different computing networks without them all having to conform to one technology. Leiner et al. (1997) gathered the recollections of many of those involved in the origins of the internet. They stressed that "the Internet as we now know it embodies a key underlying technical idea, namely that of open architecture networking. In this approach, the choice of any individual network technology was not dictated by a particular network architecture but rather could be selected freely by a provider and made to interwork with the other networks through a meta-level 'Internetworking Architecture.'"

Leiner et al.'s account continued on to explain that Robert Kahn, who developed the early internet model, the ARPANET, worked from four design principles.

- Each distinct network would have to stand on its own, and no internal changes would be required to any such network to connect it to the internet.

- Communications would be on a best effort basis. If a packet didn't make it to the final destination, then it would be retransmitted soon from the source.

- Black boxes would be used to connect the networks; they would later be called gateways and routers. There would be no information retained by the gateways about the individual flows of packets passing through them, thereby keeping them simple and avoiding complicated adaptation and recovery from various failure modes.

- There would be no global control at the operations level.

With a decentralized system, according to Baran's design, this meant that there needed to be many different connections, with no single node being more important than any other. This was realized through the network of internet routers; if one was damaged, then information could find an alternative route to its destination. An open system then followed from the decentralized approach; if the system was to have no central control, then it needed to be open so that any compatible computer and network could hook onto it and allow communication to continue.

Abstracting from these fundamentals of the internet, three core principles for robust design can be proposed for our analogy. A robust system should be

- open so that any appropriate contributor can join it;

- decentralized and thus not reliant on one central node or location; and

- distributed so that functions work throughout the network.

Turning now to education, perhaps the online pivot can be considered better as a pivot to distance education in some form in that it is focused on delivery and support to students remote from campus (or even if they are living on campus and studying from their rooms). Online delivery is how this will be realized, but distance from the physical campus, lecture hall, and exam centre is the key factor. During the pandemic, many existing distance education institutions and their students have been able to operate largely as normal. There has been disruption to some central services, such as postage and support teams, and a large-scale effect on the lives of the students living through the pandemic, but in terms of providing education it has been as near to business as normal as could be envisaged, compared with the disruption encountered by students on face-to-face campuses. Although not an ideal model, comparison of distance education to the internet can inform further consideration in making higher education as a whole more robust.

- It is distributed: students are not required to go to a central location, instead studying at home or any location of their choosing, thus making it more robust if the central location, or gathering, is compromised. It is also distributed temporally in that much of the study is conducted asynchronously. Often the distance education approach does not rely on scheduled meetings, lectures, laboratories, or seminars at specific times. This asynchronous approach allows a much greater degree of flexibility, and therefore robustness, when things become disrupted. Just as internet data packets can take different routes to their destinations, so too students can accommodate different time allocations for their studies. Distribution can also apply within the process itself, for example with assessment. By distributing assessment tasks throughout a course—using regular assignments, eportfolio tasks, self-assessments, and end-of-course projects—the assessment becomes more robust than the emphasis on a single exam. Arguably, it also becomes more pedagogically sound and relevant for students, but the focus here is on robustness.

- It is (largely) decentralized: just as students are distributed, so too the support of those students can be decentralized. This is not completely the case, for many distance education universities, such as the UKOU, have a central campus where most academic, administrative, and research staff are located. There are often smaller centres regionally, with many staff already home based or accustomed to working from home. Student support is provided by part-time tutors based all over the country and largely working from home. Thus, much of the functionality required to support students and maintain the educational purpose of the university is not placed in one central unit. In addition, modules are designed by teams and delivered through a structure rather than being reliant on one individual lecturer. Thus, it is not as reliant on any one individual for specific content as the lecture model.

- It is open: this is not necessarily a defining factor of distance education, but many providers operate an open entry policy by which students do not need to meet entry requirements from schools and colleges. The system is thus less subject to disruptions to entry procedures, for example exams and assessments in schools. Openness also plays a wider role in the use of open content and open access journals. For instance, the UKOU's OpenLearn site, which shares educational content under a Creative Commons licence, saw daily visits increase from 40,000 to over 200,000 during the pandemic (OpenLearn, 2020). This was a combination of educators wanting to learn how to deliver courses online and find material that they could repurpose and learners wanting to use time productively. Open access journals, which allow everyone to access their contents, also provide a more robust means of accessing educational content when the physical library is closed. The online pivot has seen the need for many students to access ebooks from their libraries since they could not access the physical copies. This demand has led to dramatic increases in prices from publishers to libraries for ebooks (in some cases 200%), already priced heavily for library use and with limited user licences. This has led to a campaign to investigate pricing by publishers in the United Kingdom (Hotten, 2020). Open textbooks provide a solution to vulnerability to such practices.

Distance education is also already largely online. It might not be wholly delivered this way, but there is usually an IT infrastructure, including VLE, support systems, content production, and communication tools accustomed to handling the requirements of students. As long as internet access is reliable, distance education itself is based upon a system designed to be robust. For instance, although the physical library buildings of many distance education universities might have closed during the pandemic, much of what those libraries do is already online in serving students, so the impact has been less than that of a campus library.

It is worth stressing that distance education was not designed with such robustness in mind; the usual aim was to develop an education system that would include those otherwise excluded. So, it is worth examining where weak points exist in this system also, with the goal of identifying a model for higher education more broadly.

Following are some potential risks and weaknesses of the distance education model as it is commonly realized.

- A student's home situation: the setup for students is varied. Many will have a home study arrangement in place, but some will use work-based access to computers, and if they are sent home they might lose that access.

- Home disruption: related to the above, the normal home situation will be subject to considerable disruption during a pandemic when a partner, parent, or children might also now be at home full time and require care and support.

- Internet access: the quality of home internet access can vary greatly geographically, and the costs of this provision can be shifted to students. Also, home access can deteriorate when everyone works at home and the demand increases.

- Central staff disruption: although many academic staff might have appropriate equipment and be used to working at home, many central administrative staff might not have laptops, and their work is not as easily translated online.

- Support staff: although much support work is decentralized, sometimes there are dedicated teams in physical call centres who will be affected if they need to work from home.

It is not my contention here that all higher education providers become distance education institutions; rather, the preceding analysis highlights how there are elements of robustness in the distance education model that can be modified and adapted for higher education. Ensuring more robust and reliable provision at a structural level, such that continued operation does not rely on excessive workloads for and strain on those working in higher education, seems to be one of the lessons of the online pivot.

Digital Resilience

In the previous section, I considered the idea of increasing the robustness of higher education using the design of the internet as a model. Another way to approach this in terms of metaphors is to consider the concept of resilience. The term "resilience" has been co-opted for rather dubious purposes recently. It is often closely allied with another term, "grit," that has gained prominence. Made popular by Angela Duckworth, grit is defined as "perseverance and passion for long-term goals" (Duckworth et al., 2007) and suggested as the key to being successful compared with many other traits, such as IQ. However, the term places the emphasis on the individual, excusing many of the social and structural problems that can contribute to a lack of success. The simplified version is that those in poverty just lacked sufficient "grit." In an analysis of the term, Ris (2015, p. 2) says that, "to its skeptics, grit is at best an empty buzzword, at worst a Social Darwinist explanation for why poor communities remain poor—one that blames the victims of entrenched poverty, racism, or inferior schooling for character flaws that caused their own disadvantage." Resilience is often allied with grit, as the ability to persevere through hardship and recover from setback, and has been suggested as having a positive link to mental health (Epstein & Krasner, 2013). As with grit, though, similar overtones of social Darwinism arise along with a shift of blame from society to individual.

However, before it was inveigled into such dubious usage, resilience was a useful metaphor, borrowed from ecology, and that is the interpretation that I revisit here. Referring to the stability of ecological systems, Holling (1973, p. 14) defined resilience as "a measure of the persistence of systems and of their ability to absorb change and disturbance and still maintain the same relationships between populations or state variables."

This is a much more nuanced and complex concept than grit or simply the ability to recover from setbacks. Hopkins (2009) developed Holling's (1973) definition beyond ecology as "the capacity of a system to absorb disturbance and reorganise while undergoing change, so as to retain essentially the same function, structure, identity and feedbacks." This definition emphasizes a system's overall ability to retain its function and identity, and this is relevant to our consideration of higher education post-pandemic. Consider an academic journal, which might have started as a print-based artifact, with set issues per year. Then it shifted to a combination of online and print before finally becoming online only. The editors then might have moved to a continuous publication model without set issues. They might also have made the decision to accept different forms of submissions, such as video articles. However, if the journal has retained its general aim, met the needs of the same audience, and maintained academic standards, then we would still consider it to be the same journal, but one that has changed over time, usually in response to the changing environment and perhaps the personnel on the editorial board. It has retained its core identity and as such demonstrated resilience.

Similarly, we can view the online pivot as a significant further shift to a digital system. We can think of digital resilience as a university's ability to continue its normal operations through digital means. In the previous section, I suggested that there was an over-reliance on the physical structures of universities and their functions, whereas digital resilience allows for these functions to be realized irrespective of the physical setup.

Resilience is a concept that has been applied beyond ecosystems, finding particular relevance to sustainable development and climate change (e.g., Hopkins, 2009). It has also been applied to education, and open education in particular, with Hall and Winn (2010) arguing that resilience "develops engagement, education, empowerment and encouragement. Resilient forms of HE should have the capacity to help students, staff and wider communities to develop these attributes. As technology offers reach, usability, accessibility and timely feedback, it is a key to developing a resilient higher education." Walker et al. (2004) propose four aspects of resilience that form a useful means of approaching it as a metaphor.

1. Latitude is the maximum amount that a system can be changed before losing its ability to recover.

2. Resistance is the ease or difficulty of changing the system: that is, how resistant it is to being changed.

3. Precariousness is how close the current state of the system is to a limit or "threshold."

4. Panarchy is the influences of external forces at scales above and below. For example, external oppressive politics, invasions, market shifts, or global climate change can trigger local surprises and regime shifts.

Often resilience is considered only from one of these perspectives, typically resistance. If a system is resistant to change, then it is seen as resilient. However, high resistance is not necessarily a benefit to an ecosystem, as Holling (1973) observed; for example, some insect populations fluctuate wildly depending on environmental factors but over time prove to be resilient because they have high latitude. Resilience, then, suggests adaptation to and evolution in new environmental conditions, with an emphasis on retaining the core identity of a system. In ecology, identity means that the species persists, although it might be adapted, whereas in organizational terms it means that the core functions remain, although they might be realized in newer, modified ways.

With reference to the online pivot and educational technology, resilience can be seen as utilizing technology to continue the underlying function of the institution. Although resilience can be seen at the individual level, it comes with the reservations mentioned previously, and it is perhaps best applied to the institutional level. The institution can be seen as a complex ecosystem in itself, composed of a number of individuals, behaviours, tasks, and functions.

Terry Anderson and I (Weller and Anderson, 2013) proposed adapting the four aspects of resilience (Walker et al., 2004), and for any factor of change facing a university, scoring each of them a subjective ranking of 1 to 10 (1 = low resilience, 10 = high resilience). A combined high score of more than 35 would indicate that it is a challenge for which the institution was exceptionally well adapted already, whereas a low score of less than 15 would indicate that the institution faces a considerable threat from this challenge, with which it is not well equipped to deal. We used the challenges of open access publishing and MOOCs to demonstrate the model.

However, it could also be an effective model for considering how an HEI, or higher education in general, can cope with a pandemic. Consider, for example, your own institution if you are at one. How would it score in terms of conducting the online pivot?

- Latitude: can the institution change how it teaches and still operate?

- Resistance: is there a history of adapting to change? How willing and able are staff to change how they teach and operate?

- Precariousness: what is the current state of finances, resources, and staffing?

- Panarchy: the virus is a panarchic effect in itself, but it brings with it many others, such as research funding, political shifts, changes to travel, et cetera. Different institutions will have different susceptibilities here; for example, those reliant on conferences to generate income will be affected by reductions in travel.

This exercise can then be applied to any of the longer-term post-COVID-19 scenarios. For example, versions could be used to consider continued waves of the pandemic, a serious outbreak on campus, the loss of international students, a reduction in student numbers, and so on. As a strategic exercise, this framework is worth using to indicate how ready an institution is to cope with the pandemic and where its weaknesses lie. I have found it useful to frame workshops since it will bring to the surface different perspectives from participants; whereas some will view the institution as well prepared, others will think that it is in a precarious position. Using this method can be a route to acquiring information from different components of a complex system; for example, the library might seem to be well prepared but the physical estates team under-resourced. This can then be used to identify priorities to increase the institution's overall resilience to any given scenario.

The method can also be applied to the higher education system itself, for example at a national or regional level, and it can be a tool to help set priorities and policies. Developing a more resilient system of higher education, rather than passing the burden on to individuals to develop their own resilience, is a more sustainable model. In this interpretation, I believe, resilience still has a lot to offer as a metaphor.

CHAPTER 8

Pedagogy

In this chapter, I will examine three metaphors that relate to pedagogy. The relationship with ed tech is somewhat tenuous here or at least less explicit. Each of the approaches is facilitated by ed tech but not reliant on any one technology.

Pedagogy itself is a metaphor-rich area, as noted in the introduction, and education is often framed and shaped by the underlying metaphor that someone holds for it, for example as classroom, product delivery, system, or process (Wilson, 1995). We will consider why a form of one of them is so dominant, namely the lecture, in a section of this chapter and particularly how, during the online pivot, much of the focus was on "the online lecture" as the dominant model. The first section revisits the open degree that I discussed in Chapter 2, which—though not a pedagogy in itself—is a useful example of a broader trend in designing education for increased learner choice and agency. Such a design has implications for the pedagogy adopted. The middle section provides an example of a specific metaphor used to shape the pedagogy. This is rhizomatic learning, which takes the metaphor of the rhizomatic plant to think about knowledge construction and course design.

Online pedagogies are often couched in terms of metaphors because, as we have seen, they help to frame how people operate in what can be an unfamiliar environment. During the early phases of elearning, previous pedagogies were recast as online models, for example resource-based learning and constructivism. The foundations of existing analogue models helped them to be adapted for online use. In the connectivist learning model proposed by Downes (2008) and Siemens (2005), the network itself acts as a metaphor, with people and resources forming "nodes" in a network, which Siemens defines as "the integration of principles explored by chaos, network, and complexity and self-organization theories."

One could write a whole book on pedagogical metaphors, so the coverage here is necessarily brief, but I hope that the three examples show how metaphors can affect pedagogy, with the reshaping of the context with situated agency, the direct model of rhizomes, and the reaction against a dominant metaphor with the lecture.

Situated Action and Learner Agency

In this section, I revisit the open degree program encountered in the chapter on visual metaphors. Using a metaphor of navigation, via photocopy interfaces, this acts as an example of a broader trend in flexible education and increased control and agency given to learners. Although this is not related to a specific pedagogy, or educational technology, it is an approach that requires modifications to existing pedagogical approaches and implementation through different technologies.

When the UKOU was founded, it offered only one type of degree, a BA(Open)—there were no named degrees. This was an explicit attempt by the founders of the university to make a UKOU degree different not just in mode of study but also in substance. Students constructed their own degree pathways, meaning that the courses were truly modular and could be combined as students saw fit. The UKOU's first vice-chancellor said "that a student is the best judge of what [s]he wishes to learn and that [s]he should be given the maximum freedom of choice consistent with a coherent overall pattern. They hold that this is doubly true when one is dealing with adults who, after years of experience of life, ought to be in a better position to judge what precise studies they wish to undertake" (Perry, 1976, p. 61).

Although most universities offer options and electives, a truly flexible and open structure is rare, not least because the physical instantiation of education means that timetabling creates a logistical problem. It is not possible to allow wide-ranging freedom of choice when competing courses occur at the same time in different physical spaces. Distance education, particularly when it is largely asynchronous and occurs part time over a longer period, means that students can combine courses from different areas.

Specialization, of course, is a desirable mode of study in many areas. But the reasoning behind the original open choice was that the changes in society and workplaces in the 1970s meant that a wide-ranging degree was suitable for many vocations. If that was true at the founding of the UKOU, then it is doubly so now. Although it is sensible to be skeptical of the many claims that universities are preparing students for jobs that do not exist (Doxtdator, 2017), it is also fair to say that flexibility and breadth of understanding are useful attributes in an evolving digital economy. Educational technology is a good example of this, as we saw in the chapter on whether it is a discipline or not. Although it is possible to create a degree program that covers much of what is required in the field, it is a varied domain, and much of the work involves having an appreciation of the demands of different subject areas. A degree with rich and unique variety in it might suit the needs of an educational technologist better than a dedicated one. That is increasingly true for many roles that involve the use of technology but are not necessarily purely technology focused.

It is often claimed that, in order to solve the complex, "wicked" problems that the world faces, such as sustainability, climate change, and social inclusion, interdisciplinary thinking is required (e.g., Epstein, 2019), and there has been encouragement to develop "T-shaped" students (e.g., Johnston, 1978; Oskam, 2009) who combine the depth of one subject (the vertical bar of the letter) with broader skills across disciplines (the horizontal bar). But the common structure for degree profiles continues to prioritize narrow specializations instead of encouraging students to develop knowledge and skills across a range of topics.

My intention here, though, is not to make the case for interdisciplinary, or multidisciplinary, education per se but to view variety in the degree pathway as a function of increased learner agency, in which the learner constructs their own degree profile and takes responsibility for their pathway, by way of a metaphor. To return to the open degree, then, the courses are very modular, so often they can be studied independently; that is not always the case, particularly at higher levels where some prerequisites are necessary, but nevertheless it is possible for students to construct their own degrees, which could combine art history, engineering, and music, say. Not only can students create their own pathways, but also, perhaps more importantly, they can change and adapt them as they go along, responding to changes in their lives, interests sparked by their studies, topics that they have found less interesting than expected, or shifts in society or employment. For instance, many students start on a named degree path but switch to an open one when they find other topics of interest or are less interested in their initial choices than they anticipated. For universities concerned about student retention, this flexibility offers one means of acknowledging that students can, and should be allowed to, change their minds. Although some pathways are more popular, students do combine courses in almost all of the ways imaginable, constructing unique pathways that suit them.

This responsive, agile structure of a degree program is different from conventional degree structures, which are largely predetermined. In her influential book *Plans and Situated Actions*, Suchman (1987) commences with an analogy of different forms of navigation. She uses a comparison of the Trukese and European methods of navigating the open sea: the Trukese navigator "begins with an objective rather than a plan. He sets off toward the objective and responds to conditions as they arise in an ad hoc fashion. He utilizes information provided by the wind, the waves, the tide and current, the fauna, the stars, the clouds, the sound of the water on the side of the boat, and he steers accordingly" (p. vii). The European navigator, in contrast, plots a course, "and he carries out his voyage by relating his every move to that plan. His effort throughout his voyage is directed to remaining 'on course'" (p. vii).

Suchman (1987) uses this analogy to frame how people act, in particular what she calls "situated actions," those "actions taken in the context of particular, concrete circumstances" (p. viii). In such circumstances, she contends, we act like Trukese navigators, taking in available information and (re)acting accordingly with an overall objective in mind. This is in contrast to when we have a definite plan and steps to follow. Suchman looked at how people interact with photo-copiers, where the interface is often confusing and when they do not behave how users expect them to behave. People might start with a plan, but they react and adapt, in situ, to the context. The overall goal remains the same (e.g., to get so many copies made), just as it does for Trukese navigators, but how it is achieved is determined by smaller actions that are responses to what has just occurred. Suchman suggests that this is actually how people operate much of the time, although we often talk in terms of executing plans.

This analogy works for the choice of modules in the open degree that I have outlined. This is particularly true if students are studying part time and thus over a longer period than the traditional three- or four-year full-time degree. Over this period, there is a greater chance that circumstances will change, so the degree pathway itself needs to be flexible. As an example, consider what has happened in world politics since 2016: a student might have started off with a plan for their degree but become interested in economics, or have had a career change forced on them that now requires some expertise in European politics, or might now have an idea to develop an app for their company, and so on.

This analogy for flexibility and adaptability does not apply just to the overall course structure. As Veletsianos (2019) asked, "in education, what can be made more flexible?" and correctly stated that "flexible learning most usually focus[es] on enabling learners [to gain] some degree of control and freedom over the location, time, and pace of their online studies." He proposed a number of further aspects of flexibility, including assessment in which students can choose from a menu of assignments, attendance in which students can choose to attend face-to-face or online courses, and course duration and pace in which students can vary the intensity of their study. In each example, greater agency and licence are given to learners through modifications to pedagogy. An open degree requires pedagogy that facilitates the independence of courses, while flexible assessment demands an approach that can be assessed in a variety of ways, and so on. More effort from the educator is often required, and is not without cost, but—like the Trukese navigators—this allows for a more responsive curriculum that can adapt to the increasingly complex and varied lives of many students.

From a broader open education perspective, the work of OER, open textbooks, open access, and MOOCs can all be viewed as providing the necessary foundations for a wave of more interesting exploration of what flexible approaches offer. For example, learners can take open courses and then bring this knowledge into formal study, as with the OER university model, which allows for a first-year free study then assessed formally by institutions, or how Delft universities recognize some MOOCs from other providers to offer a broader curriculum than they themselves can offer (Pickard, 2018).

There is much talk of personalization in education, and it is often portrayed as each learner being given different content within a course, often based upon analytics or artificial intelligence. But this ability within the degree structure to be responsive and adaptable—allowing students themselves to modify their approaches in response to changes—will be more significant I believe.

Rhizomes

In some parts of this book, the emphasis has been on highlighting when a metaphor is used, and what its implications are, for example in the sections "Digital Natives" and "Education Is Broken." Rhizomatic learning is a more explicit metaphor in contrast in that it shapes the approach to learning, and students are encouraged to learn the metaphor itself to appreciate how it differs from their previous experiences. In this section, I make no proposition about the value of rhizomatic learning; rather, I focus on its use as a direct pedagogical metaphor.

Rhizomatic learning gained favour following the initial MOOC phase, when educators were experimenting with different approaches that could utilize the open web, such as connectivism. Dave Cormier hosted an influential MOOC in this area, Rhizo14, an open course that itself was about rhizomatic learning. Cormier (2008) suggests rhizomatic learning as a solution to some of the problems of constructing knowledge in complex, distributed networks: "A botanical metaphor . . . may offer a more flexible conception of knowledge for the information age: the rhizome. A rhizomatic plant has no center and no defined boundary; rather, it is made up of a number of semi-independent nodes, each of which is capable of growing and spreading on its own, bounded only by the limits of its habitat."

Rhizomes spread by sending out shoots and putting down new nodes. They are often treated as weeds, and their method of spreading makes them incredibly resilient. For example, Japanese knotweed is listed as one of the most invasive species by the World Conservation Union (Lowe et al., 2000), and its strong roots can cause damage to buildings and roads. Even small segments of its rhizomes can survive and then begin to proliferate again. In this sense, the metaphor is one of robustness as well as a decentralized, connected model, but as we shall consider it might also be one of danger.

In a rhizomatic course (the term "course" might not even be appropriate), there is a good deal of negotiation between learners and facilitators. For example, though broad topic areas might be suggested, how they will be approached might be framed by questions that learners suggest. Cormier (2008) states that, "in the rhizomatic model of learning, curriculum is not driven by predefined inputs from experts; it is constructed and negotiated in real time by the contributions of those engaged in the learning process. This community acts as the curriculum, spontaneously shaping, constructing, and reconstructing itself and the subject of its learning in the same way that the rhizome responds to changing environmental conditions."

Bali et al. (2016) participated in Cormier's Rhizo14 course and provide an auto-ethnographic account. They emphasize the emergent nature of the course: that is, the constituent elements combined to create something new that was unpredictable. This was realized through connections that the participants made and content that they produced, largely through blogs. The authors report a largely positive experience and the generation of a community formed as a result of the importance placed on making connections, which persisted long after the course had finished (although, again, perhaps to talk of a start date and an end date with rhizomatic learning is inappropriate).

Others did not report such a positive experience, feeling excluded, lost, or unable to make connections (Mackness & Bell, 2015). For a course designed to have no centre, perhaps this is not surprising, but one should also recognize that many students feel this way about conventional approaches to learning.

Cormier (2014) suggests that rhizomatic learning is a method of dealing with complexity and abundant content. Beyond the courses on rhizomatic learning itself, a model from more everyday experience might be how many of us learn to operate in social media contexts such as blogs and Twitter. As with rhizomes, we make connections in these contexts, and there are clusters of people or interests operating as nodes. We learn not by formal instruction but by interaction, experimentation, negotiation, and observation of the abundant resources (in this case, other tweets, links, or blog posts). In an analysis of Twitter for the subsequent rhizomatic course, Rhiz015, Bozkurt et al. (2016) found that hashtags linked different communities and that social presence was more salient than teaching presence. That is, people were making connections and emphasizing social communication over formal pedagogical exchange. This might reflect the type of emergent learning that we all engage in when using social media.

Rhizomatic learning might be an example of a metaphor that is too explicit. Mackness and Bell (2015, p. 89) argue that "using the rhizome as a metaphor for teaching, learning, and course design requires knowledge and understanding of the theoretical principles outlined by Deleuze and Guattari (rhizome as a concept) and of the potential limitations of the metaphor for application to teaching and learning." If learners need to read Deleuze and Guattari to be able to benefit from a rhizomatic course, then that seems to require an excessive load. In this case, the rhizome metaphor behaves like the rhizome plant in a garden, taking over beyond its boundaries.

However, if the rhizome is taken at the more generative level of metaphor, then it need not be as overpowering. For example, Sanford et al. (2011) detail how video gamers learn in online communities and offer the rhizome as a means of understanding this approach to sharing and adapting. It is likely that all of the video gamers in their study were unaware of the rhizome metaphor and not explicitly trying to establish a community based upon this model. But it does offer an insight into how they were learning, and there are elements of that learning that can be adapted into more formal education.

In the section "The Problem with the Internet Trinity," we saw that many of our initial beliefs about the internet can be reinterpreted in light of the more dystopian turn that much internet use has taken. The same might be true of rhizomatic learning. Its strength as a metaphor for learning is in the resilience of the rhizome: it grows and spreads through nodes. This resilience is useful in courses such as Rhiz014, but one could also consider it as a metaphor for how misinformation spreads and why it can be so difficult to shake beliefs in conspiracy theories. Veletsianos (2021) suggested on Twitter that "rhizomatic learning is a pretty great idea, until you realize that the bamboo rhizomes in your back yard are attacking your maple tree and you're waging a losing battle against an invasive species. There's a misinformation metaphor here."

The aggressive recommendation algorithms of social media platforms such as Pinterest, YouTube, and Facebook act as the spreading rhizomes, until a stable structure is established, which will survive the removal of any one node. We have seen during the pandemic that belief in anti-vaccination conspiracies has proven to be very stubborn despite any one claim being debunked. This is in part because of a rhizomatic form of "learning" that the conspiracy theorist has undertaken, facilitated by the algorithms of social media. This is to suggest not that rhizomatic learning is therefore a "bad" metaphor for learning but that it can offer insights into how to combat such harmful conspiracy theories, against which conventional approaches to education have struggled.

The Lecture and Online Education

The lecture might seem to be an odd choice as a metaphor because in most instances we mean it literally: students attend lectures in a lecture hall. But for online learning, it has served as a model that is either replicated or presented in terms of its difference. This became particularly apparent during the online pivot, in which the lecture was deemed the only, and best, method to realize higher education. All online options were then presented as attempts to recreate lectures online or as deficit models compared with face-to-face lectures.

When Cambridge University announced that it was moving online, the headline was "All Lectures to Be Online-Only" (BBC News, 2020).

Not that all learning was moving online, but the stress was on lectures. There was a call that students should be offered refunds because they might deem online learning inferior (Palfreyman & Farrington, 2020). The UK education secretary reportedly demanded that universities should resume face-to-face lectures or have their funding cut (Neilan, 2021). *The Sunday Times* ran the headline "Universities Refuse to End Online Lessons" (Griffiths, 2021), with the implication that online learning should be stopped as soon as possible. Others went even further, declaring distance education and online learning to be an existential threat: "Continuing with virtual learning threatens the entire concept of the college experience. Higher education, like K-12, depends on proximity to real people, not squares on a screen. Educators at all levels have dedicated themselves to teaching students during the pandemic, but they know that they're offering thin pedagogical gruel. . . . The main reason why the 'distance learning revolution' didn't replace the traditional model is that online learning just isn't as good" (Laporte & Cassuto, 2020).

Figlio et al. (2013) compared face-to-face lectures with streamed online versions and found that students preferred the face-to-face versions. This is perhaps unsurprising, rather like comparing the live performance of theatre to seeing it on television. But the comparison is unfair if it is meant to demonstrate that online learning is inferior. This is clearly not learning designed to be taken online, so it always suffers in comparison. Courses designed specifically for online delivery make use of the affordances of that medium, such as a rich mix of resources, asynchronous delivery, embedded communication and commentary, and so on. To return to the theatre analogy, the comparison would be not with theatre streamed to television but with a more internet-native form of entertainment, such as online gaming. The desired outcome for people who partake of both is similar—to be entertained—but the environments in which this goal is realized offer different possibilities.

During the early stages of the online pivot, it was understandable that the lecture was the means by which higher education could provide a continuation of service. There simply was not time to do anything else. Hill (2020) suggested that the online pivot would go through different stages.

- Phase 1 (February–March 2020): rapid transition to remote teaching and learning

- Phase 2 (April–July 2020): (re)adding the basics

- Phase 3 (August–December 2020): extended transition during continued turmoil

- Phase 4 (2021 and beyond): emerging new normal

It is likely that in Hill's model only at Phase 4, when online and blended provision becomes part of the normal offering, even when the pandemic is over, will we see extensive course redesign.

These objections to online learning maintain the central belief in the superiority of the lecture. Indeed, it seems that no other model is imaginable. With that basis, online learning becomes a mere replication of the lecture, and inevitably this is seen as a deficit. Even in this limited frame, there is some room for debate since lecture capture (in which a face-to-face lecture is recorded and can be viewed by students at any time) has been in place for some time on many campuses. The results are varied, but it can lead to a decline in attendance (Morris et al., 2019), which prompts the question that, if the face-to-face experience is unarguably superior, then why do students opt to watch lectures online? They might do so for a variety of reasons, including convenience, improved note taking, and controlled pace of the lecture. In short, the kind of flexibility that asynchronous online learning can offer compared with synchronous face-to-face learning, but lecture capture really hints only at the difference rather than an approach designed specifically for online delivery.

What this reliance on the lecture demonstrates is a paucity of metaphors or models for other ways of learning. The default metaphor becomes the lecture because that is all that people have experienced. How did the lecture get to this position of dominance as the sole measure of pedagogical excellence? As a means of knowledge transmission, it is not that effective generally, with Laurillard (2001, p. 93) concluding that it is "a very unreliable way of transferring the lecturer's knowledge to the student's notes." She goes on to decry the persistence of the lecture despite this inefficiency: "Why aren't lectures scrapped as a teaching method? If we forget the eight hundred years of university tradition that legitimises them, and imagine starting afresh with the problem of how to enable a large percentage of the population to understand difficult and complex ideas, I doubt that lectures will immediately spring to mind as the obvious solution" (p. 93).

Partly, the lecture's continuation is a result of cultural inertia. As Laurillard (2001) points out, there are some 800 years of history that are hard to overcome. Students are taught via lectures, and when they become educators that is the model that they know and perpetuate. It is also true that lectures can be effective means of combining different media such as video, image, text, and spoken word. They are also performances that the learner participates in, along with others, making them social events (Friesen, 2014). And, despite Laurillard's objections to the format overall, we can all cite examples of highly effective lectures.

In addition to social inertia, there is an economic model for lectures. Online learning can offer cost savings (Battaglino et al., 2012), but often this is through the sort of reduced labour models highlighted in the section "Uber for Education." Developing online learning nearly always turns out to be more expensive than anticipated, as evident from much of the investment in MOOCs (Hollands & Tirthali, 2014). Cost saving is not the best reason to pursue online learning, although it is not necessarily more expensive than constructing a campus and maintaining physical buildings. However, once those construction costs have been paid, there is an economic argument for continuing with the lecture model. Although the campus-based lecture model is not necessarily more cost effective than the purely online model, and vice versa, they do involve different types of costs. For example, online learning typically requires more investment in course production than a face-to-face lecture series, whereas the campus model necessitates building and maintenance costs. It therefore becomes expensive to run both specialized online learning and campus-based learning simultaneously since they have different cost requirements.

It has been the case for many years that universities have offered a form of blended, or hybrid, learning that combines some face-to-face and online elements. A model that has gained popularity during the pandemic is that of hyflex (Beatty, 2007), combining the terms "hybrid" and "flexible," in which students can attend face-to-face lectures or online lectures, giving them flexibility. Irvine (2020) notes the semantic confusion among online, remote, blended, flexible, and hybrid learning, making comparisons difficult, and stresses that pedagogy is separate from modality. However, if the lecture is taken as the basic model for online and, by extension, blended learning, then a number of assumptions follow.

- Education is largely based upon synchronous lectures.

- It deploys a one-to-many model.

- It uses a largely didactic pedagogy.

- The significance of timetabling for interdisciplinary study is reinforced.

An online course, in contrast, can be asynchronous, so the learner can control the time when and the place where she engages in study. It can be collaborative in a variety of ways, for example by creating shared documents or wikis, aggregating blog posts together, sharing found resources, commenting on a peer's work, engaging in discussion on course content, annotating web pages, editing an open textbook, et cetera. All of these tasks can be done face to face also, but by shifting online and combining synchronous and asynchronous elements many of the tasks are easier to achieve. The asynchronous, online approach also allows for the multidisciplinary study and flexibility that arise when timetabling becomes less significant. Shifting away from the lecture as the central model creates space both cognitively and in the course study calendar for such approaches to be explored.

The architecture of the university campus shapes much of how higher education is realized. It undertakes a significant amount of the labour required in terms of organization for students and staff: they arrive at a certain place at a certain time to receive content (the lecture); they go to another place for discussion (a seminar), another location for laboratory work, a separate building to access resources (the library); they undertake socialization in cafés and bars designed to promote it. When learning shifts online, these cues are lost, with two consequences: the learner must take on more responsibility to organize their own learning, and the educator must explicitly build these different types of interaction into the course design. The architecture no longer performs much of the implicit work, but this is also liberating. Following are some examples from my own experience.

- Group activities that can be done quickly face to face take much more time online, particularly if they involve allocating roles and tasks to people.

- In online discussion forums, it can be the case that people who do not often speak up in class have more to say.

- Instructions and contents that might seem to be obvious will not be to some learners. If something can be misinterpreted, then inevitably it will be, so using critical readers prior to delivery is important.

- Once a mistaken belief takes hold, it is very difficult to rectify, much more so than in face-to-face learning, so it needs to be dealt with quickly.

- Students will study at different times, with different amounts of material, and at different paces.

- Social interaction can be achieved with as much significance for its participants as face-to-face social bonds, and students will often self-organize to realize this, for example via Facebook or in forums designed for other purposes.

- A distant, aloof air in a face-to-face lecture will seem to be even more cold and remote online.

- It is more important to structure different types of activity explicitly to maintain engagement.

- Peer-to-peer interaction needs to be designed more explicitly with clear outcomes.

There are different considerations in each mode, and if possible some blend might well be beneficial; for example, initial face-to-face meetings to start group projects can save a lot of time. The dominance of the lecture metaphor often prevents such consideration from occurring since it represents the starting point rather than one possible element in a mix. The lecture is so entrenched that many do not perceive it as a metaphor when considering an online design. This is a feature of metaphors: they shape our responses to a new environment. Martínez et al. (2001, p. 966) sum this up with respect to educational metaphors, stating that "we may not be aware of the pervasive influence under which we act, because our prevailing metaphors usually represent the undisputed state of the art in our community of practice." This seems to be the case with the lecture, but perhaps as we enter later phases of the online pivot there will be a more sector-wide shift to reframe the discussion.

Using Metaphor Appropriately

In this book, we have explored many different metaphors, and no doubt some will have been more successful than others. The metaphors have focused on different aspects of educational technology, with the online pivot arising from the COVID-19 pandemic being a recurring theme. Before considering the nature of metaphors used in this book, then, let us consider how we might approach ed tech in its more central, pivotal role. As I have argued, higher education as a system needs to reflect on the lessons from the online pivot and develop a means of improving its overall resilience without relying on unsustainable expectations among those working within it. Developing an approach to ed tech that promotes its central role while maintaining an appropriately critical and ethical stance to its use will be key to developing this resilience.

One way of thinking about this is to imagine that you are in charge of a fund to procure educational technology or, if you prefer, responsible for such a budget at your institution. What would be your principles or criteria for determining which ones to procure? From the analysis in this book and the lessons that we can draw from the metaphors, following is an attempt at defining such an approach.

Treat ed tech implementation like research. Start with definite research hypotheses, such as "implementing this will improve student retention by 5%." Developing such hypotheses will both focus attention on what the technology can do for students and inform the institution if it is actually realizing these aims. In the sections on "Blockchain and Alchemy" and "The Ed Tech Rapture," I argued that often claims made about technology are couched in terms of fear or revolution. Developing a more practical evidence-based approach acts as an antidote to much of this rhetoric.

Consider social impacts of technology. Ask questions such as where does this technology come from? What will be the impacts on students and educators? Technology does not exist in a social vacuum, and, as the section on "Castell Coch and the Lure of Ed Tech" illustrates, there is a strong appeal in education to many technology companies, so investigating the motives is important. The "VAR and Learning Analytics" section emphasizes the human element in education, and the impacts that technology can have on behaviour, attitude, and satisfaction are significant considerations.

Track the data implications. Related to the previous point, questions that all institutions should ask about technology pertain to data, such as what data does the institution generate? Who owns the data? How will the data be used?

Avoid hype and question metaphors. The chapter on "Ed Tech Criticism" focused on how metaphor and language are used to frame the contexts of solutions. As soon as anyone mentions disruption, revolution, transformation, and so on, suspicions should be raised. To return to the first item on this list, the use of such terms is usually a disguise for not having a clear, testable, and therefore falsifiable benefit.

Focus on achievable goals within a year. Related to the above, if the technology is capable of an improvement, then it should be demonstrable within a year. It might be modest at this stage, but some initial findings will be detectable.

Avoid inverse investment scrutiny. Ed tech often suffers from an inverse scrutiny problem. If an educator wants to try something small scale and experimental with one class, then she has to justify every aspect of it. If the institution wants to invest millions of dollars, then vague goals and rhetoric are sufficient. This should be flipped around, as I argued in the section "Rewilding Ed Tech," and small-scale experiments—lightweight and without some of the testing constraints that I am listing here—should be encouraged. Institutional structures should allow for the type of guerrilla research set out in the section "Hussites and Guerrilla Research." Conversely, large-scale investments need to be clear about what they intend to achieve and why.

Give educators and learners agency. Tools that help educators to teach more effectively or in different ways and thus help their students will be received with more enthusiasm than those that seek to make them redundant. Technology that reduces the role of an educator or makes teaching feel less worthwhile is a losing proposition from the start. Similarly, structures and technologies that give agency and control to students can aid their sense of engagement in the educational process.

Talk in educational terms. Students are not customers or data points. Learning is not a marketplace transaction. Much of this language is transferred from the technology sector, for example with Uber-type approaches to education. Ed tech projects should communicate in a language that is meaningful to students and educators.

Address sustainability and reproducibility. With significant investment and attention, it is always possible to gain some benefit. It is worth asking if that effect will still be present 5 years from now and for different students. There is a caveat, though; if you are targeting a specific group, for example students with disabilities, then it does not need to be applicable to all learners.

Appreciate student diversity. Not all learners are the same. What works for some will be despised by others, what is easy for one student will be a barrier to another with a different set of needs, and what is helpful in one place is interfering in another. As in the section "VLE/LMS," there needs to be a balance between allowing diversity and experimentation while maintaining robust systems for students.

Reward appropriate work. Often a technology-related approach will succeed on a small scale, and the credit will be given to the technology, but it arises in fact from a substantial amount of hidden labour. As the section "Hidden Labour and Hunter-Gatherers in Open Practice" highlighted, effort is required to bring to the surface, recognize, and reward such labour, particularly as it relates to care and support.

Recognize educational technologists. One common complaint among educational technologists is that often universities don't know quite what to do with them. If you look at where learning technology units are placed in organizational structures, then this uncertainty is highlighted: sometimes they are aligned with the library, other times they are part of IT, or within the Faculty of Education, or perhaps under the direct aegis of a Vice Principal. As technology is increasingly viewed as the means by which strategic change is realized, and its significance has increased, where such units sit and what they do are subject to political, financial, and tactical changes by senior management. Learning technology units often perform a strange mix of functions, and this varies across different institutions, so there is no agreed structure. In some institutions, they are service units, responsible for ensuring things such as lecture capture and VLE work. In others, they might also have a role in designing learning, or researching new technology, or being experts in pedagogy, or undertaking staff development in technology. The chapter on "Ed Tech as an Undiscipline" highlighted its diverse nature and different approaches to it, but trusting members of the unit, giving them stability, and involving them in decisions are ways to address the issue of rootlessness.

Know your metaphors. Finally, I hope that this book has raised the significance of metaphors when approaching the area of ed tech. Fundamentally, how people conceive of the relationship between education and technology will be couched in metaphors. It is worth raising them explicitly, including your own. Often they are unacknowledged, for example with the lecture as a model for online education. In turn, using new metaphors can generate new insights into and understandings of ed tech.

Metaphors are a means of approaching each of these recommendations. In this book, a range of such metaphors has been proposed. Undoubtedly, they will not be the metaphors that you would have chosen. I am not an expert scholar in subjects as diverse as Welsh history, Hussite rebellion, hunter-gatherer anthropology, or rewilding ecology, but I hope to have given these subjects sufficient details (though not drowning them in excessive details) to be useful as metaphors and enough depth to be respectful to the topic. Experts in these subjects undoubtedly will be able to point to simplifications or absences that would change or invalidate the metaphors. I accept this problem and apologize to those experts, but I would argue that the metaphors are still useful and valid for most readers. The diversity of metaphors in this book is an attempt to demonstrate that almost anything can be a metaphor, although not necessarily a useful one. The range is also intended to highlight that, for those working in ed tech, often they will have to work with people from different disciplines. Using metaphors from their own disciplines can improve engagement with, and understanding of, ed tech, and hopefully some of the metaphors in this book will provide inspiration for such an approach. My intention in this book is to reveal some insights into ed tech and to highlight the power of metaphors (and language more broadly) in how we shape our relationships with it. If you accept my contention at the start of the book that ed tech, particularly since the pandemic, will play a central role in how higher education will be realized in the future, then developing tools for thinking about it, questioning its role, assessing the motives of those behind it, and deploying it for the benefit of learners will be increasingly important for everyone involved in education.

Metaphors are powerful tools, but that does not mean that they are always beneficial. They should be approached with caution. I set out a number of examples of how metaphors have been used to frame the problems of education to the benefit of interested parties. In addition to this dubious deployment of metaphors, they can exclude people. Metaphors often gain their power from a shared understanding of the base domain. However, this can also be a drawback to their use. For example, if I use a metaphor of a children's television program that I watched as a child, then it would appeal to those who remember that program but exclude those who are too young or from different cultural backgrounds. In my selection of metaphors, it is impossible to remove the self from their influence and range. If you live in Kenya or Fiji, say, then undoubtedly there will be metaphors related to local customs, food, entertainment, politics, or geography that will be more powerful for people in that context. This is both the power and the issue with metaphors. As Loveless (2019, p. 13) puts it, "all I can hope is that what is missing does not overshadow what is present, and that the claims at the heart of this book come across with respect and care."

In this book, different types of metaphors have been used and put to different purposes, including

- a means of thinking about the deployment of new technology (e.g., "VAR and Learning Analytics");

- where we should exercise caution about the motives of proponents (e.g., "Castell Coch and Ed Tech Investment");

- how a problem is framed to suit those with a particular agenda (e.g., "Education Is Broken");

- the nature of educational technology as a field (e.g., "Digital Mudlarking");

- the nature of open practice (e.g., "Hidden Labour and Hunter-Gatherers in Open Practice");

- how research can be conducted and shared (e.g., "Hussites and Guerrilla Research");

- how to approach the impact of external events such as the COVID-19 pandemic (e.g., "Digital Resilience"); and

- a method for rethinking online pedagogy (e.g., "Rhizomes").

If any of these purposes is relevant to your practice, then I would argue that metaphors provide a means for working through the complex issues surrounding each of them. They might not provide a perfect solution, but they do offer a "mental sandpit" in which to explore issues from different perspectives. Given the central role that ed tech will play in much of higher education, developing this skill will help to improve our relationships with it, and I hope that this book goes a little way toward aiding that. Ed tech is not going away, but that doesn't mean that we are powerless before it. Perhaps most of all I hope that what the metaphors in this book have illustrated is that it is possible to be creative and imaginative in our relationships with technology. Particularly during the pandemic, this relationship often has been reduced to the utilitarian and pragmatic. Although they are important considerations, there is also room for creativity, excitement, and even enjoyment in how we think and therefore deploy technology in education. Metaphors provide an alternative way of approaching technology beyond the demands of spreadsheets, budgets, and roadmaps that allows for greater flexibility and freedom in how we conceive of its implementation. Ultimately, how ed tech is developed, used, and questioned will be essential for its humane implementation.

REFERENCES

Adams, R. (2013, April 23). Sal Khan: The man who tutored his cousin—and started a revolution. *The Guardian*. https://www.theguardian.com/education/2013/apr/23/sal-khan-academy-tutored-educational-website

Amnesty International. (2018). *Toxic Twitter—A toxic place for women*. https://www.amnesty.org/en/latest/research/2018/03/online-violence-against-women-chapter-1/

Andersen, J. P., Nielsen, M. W., Simone, N. L., Lewiss, R. E., & Jagsi, R. (2020, June 15). Meta-research: COVID-19 medical papers have fewer women first authors than expected. *Elife, 9*, Article e58807. https://doi.org/10.7554/eLife.58807

Anderson, A., Huttenlocher, D., Kleinberg, J., & Leskovec, J. (2014, April). Engaging with massive online courses. In *Proceedings of the 23rd International Conference on World Wide Web* (pp. 687–698).

Anderson, B. (2006). *Imagined communities: Reflections on the origin and spread of nationalism*. Verso Books.

Anderson, J. (2019, May 28). Investors are betting the Netflix of education can give kids what schools can't. *Quartz*. https://qz.com/1625384/spanish-with-taylor-swift-potions-with-harry-potter-outschool-wants-kids-to-pursue-their-passions/

Andrews, P. (2001). *The house book*. Phaidon.

Arora, P. (2010). Hope-in-the-wall? A digital promise for free learning. *British Journal of Educational Technology, 41*, 689–702. https://bera-journals.onlinelibrary.wiley.com/doi/abs/10.1111/j.1467-8535.2010.01078.x

Bailey, J. (2020, June 16). "Jaws": The shifting models of masculinity in Steven Spielberg's blockbuster. *The Playlist*. https://theplaylist.net/jaws-essay-45th-anniversary-20200616/

Bali, M. (2015, April 20). Pedagogy of care—Gone massive. *Hybrid Pedagogy*. https://hybridpedagogy.org/pedagogy-of-care-gone-massive/

Bali, M. (2020, May 28). Pedagogy of care: COVID-19 edition. *Hybrid Pedagogy*. https://blog.mahabali.me/educational-technology-2/pedagogy-of-care-covid-19-edition/

Bali, M., Honeychurch, S., Hamon, K., Hogue, R., Koutropoulos, S., Johnson, S., Leunissen, R., & Singh, L. (2016). What is it like to learn and participate in rhizomatic MOOCs? A collaborative autoethnography of #RHIZO14. *Current*

Issues in Emerging eLearning, 3(1), Article 4. https://scholarworks.umb.edu/ciee/vol3/iss1/4

Barber, M., Donnelly, K., Rizvi, S., & Summers, L. (2013). *An avalanche is coming: Higher education and the revolution ahead.* The Institute of Public Policy Research.

Barnum, M. (2019, April 1). The Chan Zuckerberg Initiative has made over $100 million in education grants since 2018, new disclosure shows. *Chalkbeat.* https://www.chalkbeat.org/posts/us/2019/04/01/chan-zuckerberg-initiative-100-million-education-grants-disclosure/

Batelle, J. (2016, July 13). Max Ventilla of AltSchool: The full shift dialogs transcript. *NewCo. Shift.* https://shift.newco.co/2016/07/13/max-ventilla-of-altschool-the-full-shift-dialogs-transcript/

Bates, T. (2020). Defining the affordances of face-to-face teaching. *GASTA.me.* http://gasta.me/tony-bates/

Battaglino, T. B., Haldeman, M., & Laurans, E. (2012). The costs of online learning. *Education Reform for the Digital Era, 1,* 1–13.

BBC News. (2016, November 16). "Post-truth" declared word of the year by *Oxford Dictionaries.* https://www.bbc.co.uk/news/uk-37995600

BBC News. (2020, May 19). Cambridge University: All lectures to be online-only until summer of 2021. https://www.bbc.co.uk/news/education-52732814

Beatty, B. J. (2007). Hybrid classes with flexible participation options—If you build it, how will they come? In *AECT 2007 annual proceedings—Anaheim* (vol., 15, pp. 15–24).

Beetham, H. (2005). E-portfolios in post-16 learning in the UK: Developments, issues and opportunities. http://bectaepexpert.pbworks.com/f/Beetham+eportfolio_ped.doc

Belkin, D., & Thurm, S. (2012, December 28). Dean's list: Hiring spree fattens college bureaucracy—and tuition. *Wall Street Journal.* https://www.wsj.com/articles/SB10001424127887323316804578161490716042814

Bellas, M. L. (1999). Emotional labor in academia: The case of professors. *The Annals of the American Academy of Political and Social Science, 561*(1), 96–110.

Bennett, S., Maton, K., & Kervin, L. (2008). The "digital natives" debate: A critical review of the evidence. *British Journal of Educational Technology, 39*(5), 775–786.

Blanchflower, D. G., & Oswald, A. J. (1998). What makes an entrepreneur? *Journal of Labor Economics, 16*(1), 26–60.

Bohannon, J. (2016, April 28). Who's downloading pirated papers? Everyone. *Science.* https://www.sciencemag.org/news/2016/04/whos-downloading-pirated-papers-everyone

Borsay, P. (1989) *The English urban renaissance: Culture and society in the provincial town 1660–1770.* Oxford University Press.

Botha, E. (2009). Why metaphor matters in education. *South African Journal of Education, 29*(4), 431–444.

Bothwell, E. (2018, September 6). THE developing ranking based on Sustainable Development Goals. *Times Higher Education.* https://www.times highereducation.com/news/developing-ranking-based-sustainable -development-goals

Bourg, C. (2018, April 17). Open as in dangerous. *Feral Librarian.* https://chrisbourg .wordpress.com/2018/04/17/open-as-in-dangerous/

Bowles, K. (2019, April 10). A quilt of stars: Time, work and open pedagogy. *Keynote OER19 Conference.* https://oer19.oerconf.org/sessions/welcome-from-the-co -chairs-and-keynote-by-kate-bowles/

Boyle, J. (1997). Foucault in cyberspace: Surveillance, sovereignty, and hardwired censors. https://law.duke.edu/boylesite/foucault.htm

Bozkurt, A., Honeychurch, S., Caines, A., Bali, M., Koutropoulos, A., & Cormier, D. (2016). Community tracking in a cMOOC and nomadic learner behavior identification on a connectivist rhizomatic learning network. *Turkish Online Journal of Distance Education, 17*(4), 4–30.

Bump, J. K. (2018). Fertilizing riparian forests: Nutrient repletion across ecotones with trophic rewilding. *Philosophical Transactions of the Royal Society B: Biological Sciences, 373* (1761): 20170439. http://dx.doi.org/10.1098/rstb.2017.0439

Buranyi, S. (2017, June 27). Is the staggeringly profitable business of scientific publishing bad for science? *The Guardian.* https://www.theguardian.com/science/ 2017/jun/27/profitable-business-scientific-publishing-bad-for-science

Burg, J., Murphy, C., & Pétraud, J. (2018, November 29). Blockchain for international development: Using a learning agenda to address knowledge gaps. *MERL Tech.* http://merltech.org/blockchain-for-international-development-using -a-learning-agenda-to-address-knowledge-gaps/

Burke, L. (2015, February 5). Wanted: Uber-ized education. *The Heritage Foundation.* https://www.heritage.org/education/commentary/wanted-uber-ized -education

Calderon, A. (2018). *Massification of higher education revisited.* RMIT University. https://www.researchgate.net/publication/331521091_Massification_of_higher _education_revisited

Canetti, E. (1962). *Crowds and power* (C. Stewart, Trans.). Macmillan.

Caputi, J. (2010). *Jaws* as patriarchal myth. *Journal of Popular Film, 6*(4), 305–326. https://doi.org/10.1080/00472719.1978.9943447

Caulfield, M. (2017, November 21). Traces #33: Pizza laundering. https:// hapgood.us/2017/11/21/traces-33-pizza-laundering/

Caulfield, M. (2019, June 19). SIFT—The four moves. https://hapgood.us/2019/ 06/19/sift-the-four-moves/

Cellan-Jones, R. (2018, October 2). Could blockchain solve Irish border issue? *BBC News.* https://www.bbc.co.uk/news/technology-45725572

Cellini, B. (1728). The casting of Perseus. *Vita.* https://www.bartleby.com/library/ prose/1252.html

Christensen, C. (1997). *The innovator's dilemma.* Harvard Business School Press.

Christensen, C., Johnson, C., & Horn, M. (2009). *Disrupting class: How disruptive innovation will change the way the world learns.* McGraw-Hill.

Christensen, G., Steinmetz, A., Alcorn, B., Bennett, A., Woods, D., & Emanuel, E. (2013, November 6). The MOOC phenomenon: Who takes massive open online courses and why? https://doi.org/10.2139/ssrn.2350964

Clow, D. (2010, July 14). Scott Leslie: Open educator as DJ. https://dougclow.org/2010/07/14/scott-leslie-open-educator-as-dj/

Cole, M. (1999). Cellini's blood. *The Art Bulletin, 81*(2), 215–235. https://www.tandfonline.com/doi/abs/10.1080/00043079.1999.10786883

Conkey, M. W. (2003). Has feminism changed archaeology? *Signs: Journal of Women in Culture and Society, 28*(3), 867–880.

Cooke, H., Lane, A., and Taylor, P. (2018). Open by degrees: A case of flexibility or personalization? In C. Stevenson (Ed.), *Enhancing education through open degree programs and prior learning assessment* (pp.128–148). IGI Global.

Corcoran, B. (2018, December 11). How Google's former China chief thinks AI will reshape teaching. *EdSurge.* https://www.edsurge.com/news/2018-12-11-how-this-famed-chinese-venture-capitalist-thinks-ai-will-reshape-teaching

Cormier, D. (2008). Rhizomatic education: Community as curriculum. *Innovate: Journal of Online Education, 4*(5).

Cormier, D. (2014). Rhizo14—The MOOC that community built. *Innovation and Quality in Learning, 107.*

Coretti, C. (2015). *Cellini's Perseus and Medusa and the Loggia dei Lanzi: Configurations of the body of state.* Brill.

Costa, C. (2016). Double gamers: Academics between fields. *British Journal of Sociology of Education, 37*(7), 993–1013.

Cronin, C. (2017). Openness and praxis: Exploring the use of open educational practices in higher education. *The International Review of Research in Open and Distributed Learning, 18*(5). https://doi.org/10.19173/irrodl.v18i5.3096

Crook, J. M. (1981). *William Burges and the high Victorian dream.* Frances Lincoln.

Cruse, L. R., Eckerson, E., & Gault, B. (2018). Understanding the new college majority: The demographic and financial characteristics of independent students and their postsecondary outcomes (Briefing Paper IWPR #C462). *Institute for Women's Policy Research.* https://iwpr.org/iwpr-general/understanding-the-new-college-majority-the-demographic-and-financial-characteristics-of-independent-students-and-their-postsecondary-outcomes/

Cuen, L. (2017, June 2). Diversity in tech: Open source networks have a sexism problem. *International Business Times.* https://www.ibtimes.com/diversity-tech-open-source-networks-have-sexism-problem-2547192

Czerniewicz, L. (2018, October). Unbundling and rebundling higher education in an age of inequality. *Educause Review.* https://er.educause.edu/articles/2018/10/unbundling-and-rebundling-higher-education-in-an-age-of-inequality

Dahlberg, F. (Ed.). (1981). *Woman the gatherer.* Yale University Press.

Daspin, E. (2015, July 13). Why this controversial former CNN host is launching an education news site. *Fortune*. https://fortune.com/2015/07/13/why-this -controversial-former-cnn-host-is-launching-an-education-news-site/

Davies, G. (2018, October 3). World's 1st blockchain university to begin teaching in 2019. *ABC News*. https://abcnews.go.com/International/worlds-1st-blockchain -university-begin-teaching-2019/story?id=58226066

Davies, J. (1981). *Cardiff and the marquesses of Bute*. University of Wales Press.

Davis, A. (2015, June 8). Rewilding education. *Read Write Respond*. https://read writerespond.com/2015/06/rewilding-education/

Deepwell, M. (2020, January 26). Four: The travelling monument kit. https:// marendeepwell.com/?p=2501

DeMillo, R. (2019, October 13). How blockchain technology will disrupt higher education. *The Chronicle of Higher Education*. https://www.chronicle.com/article/ how-blockchain-technology-will-disrupt-higher-education/

Donvito, T. (2021, November 18). 20 things millennials have been killing off in the last decade. *Reader's Digest*. https://www.rd.com/culture/things-millennials -have-killed/

Downes, S. (2008). Places to go: Connectivism and connective knowledge. *Innovate: Journal of Online Education, 5*(1), 1–6.

Downes, S. (2014, March 21). Like reading a newspaper. *Half an Hour*. https:// halfanhour.blogspot.com/2014/03/like-reading-newspaper.html

Doxtdator, B. (2017, July 8). A field guide to "jobs that don't exist yet." *BD: Essays on the Intersection of Politics and Pedagogy*. https://longviewoneducation.org/ field-guide-jobs-dont-exist-yet/

Duckworth, A. L., Peterson, C., Matthews, M. D., & Kelly, D. R. (2007). Grit: Perseverance and passion for long-term goals. *Journal of Personality and Social Psychology, 92* (6), 1087–1101.

Encyclopaedia Britannica. (2006). Apocalypticism. https://www.britannica.com/ topic/apocalypticism

Epstein, D. (2019). *Range: Why generalists triumph in a specialized world*. Penguin.

Epstein, R. M., & Krasner, M. S. (2013). Physician resilience: What it means, why it matters, and how to promote it. *Academic Medicine, 88*(3), 301–303.

Erdley, D. (2013). Administrative growth drives up costs at state-owned universities. *TribLive*. https://archive.triblive.com/news/pennsylvania/administrative -growth-drives-up-costs-at-state-owned-universities/#axzz2rxjtBzai

Facebook. (2021). *Enabling learning communities*. https://education.facebook.com/

Fagan, N. (2018, August). Universities use blockchain to streamline student services. *EdTech Magazine*. https://edtechmagazine.com/higher/article/2018/08/ universities-use-blockchain-streamline-student-services

Farrelly, T., Costello, E., & Donlon, E. (2020). VLEs: A metaphorical history from sharks to limpets. *Journal of Interactive Media in Education, 2020*(1).

Farry, W. (2020). The problems created by VAR are worse than those it was designed to solve. *Joe*. https://www.joe.co.uk/sport/var-decisions-football-235705

FemEdTech. (2020). Open letter to editors/editorial boards. https://femedtech.net/published/open-letter-to-editors-editorial-boards/

Figlio, D., Rush, M., & Yin, L. (2013). Is it live or is it internet? Experimental estimates of the effects of online instruction on student learning. *Journal of Labor Economics, 31*(4), 763–784.

Ford, K. C., Veletsianos, G., & Resta, P. (2014). The structure and characteristics of #PhDChat, an emergent online social network. *Journal of Interactive Media in Education, 1*, Article 8. https://doi.org/10.5334/2014-08

Ford, M. (2015). *Rise of the robots: Technology and the threat of a jobless future.* Basic Books.

Frentz, T. S., & Rushing, J. H. (1993). Integrating ideology and archetype in rhetorical criticism, part II: A case study of *Jaws. Quarterly Journal of Speech, 79*(1), 61–81.

Friesen, N. (2014). A brief history of the lecture: A multi-media analysis. *Medien-Pädagogik: Zeitschrift für Theorie, und Praxis der Medienbildung, 24*, 136–153.

Fudge, T. A. (1998). "Neither mine nor thine": Communist experiments in Hussite Bohemia. *Canadian Journal of History, 33*(1), 25–47.

Fudge, T. A. (2013). *The trial of Jan Hus: Medieval heresy and criminal procedure.* Oxford University Press.

Furedi, F. (2018, June 28). Universities' risk aversion is hampering intellectual progress. *Times Higher Education.* https://www.timeshighereducation.com/opinion/universities-risk-aversion-hampering-intellectual-progress

Galea-Pace, S. (2019). University of Bahrain set to become one of first universities to issue digital diplomas anchored to blockchain. *Business Chief.* https://middleeast.businesschief.com/leadership/2246/University-of-Bahrain-set-to-become-one-of-first-universities-to-issue-digital-diplomas-anchored-to-blockchain

Gardner, C. C., & Gardner, G. J. (2015). Bypassing interlibrary loan via Twitter: An exploration of #icanhazpdf requests. In *Proceedings of ACRL 2015, Portland, Oregon.* http://eprints.rclis.org/24847/

Gates Foundation. (2021). *Global education program.* https://www.gatesfoundation.org/our-work/programs/global-growth-and-opportunity/global-education-program

Gentner, D. (1989). The mechanisms of analogical reasoning. In S, Vosniadou & A. Ortony (Eds.). *Similarity and analogical reasoning.* Cambridge University Press.

Gerard, D. (2019, May 26). Woolf, the university on the blockchain—or not. https://davidgerard.co.uk/blockchain/2019/05/26/woolf-the-university-on-the-blockchain-or-not/

Gourlay, L. (2015). Open education as a "heterotopia of desire." *Learning, Media and Technology, 40*(3), 310–327.

Gozzi, R. Jr. (1999). *The power of metaphor in the age of electronic media.* Hampton Press.

Grech, A., & Camilleri, A. F. (2017). *Blockchain in education*. Joint Research Center. https://publications.europa.eu/en/publication-detail/-/publication/fe2e2bc8-c500-11e7-9b01-01aa75ed71a1/language-en

Greene, P. (2019, July 15). What can we learn from an experimental high tech wunder-school failure? *Forbes*. https://www.forbes.com/sites/petergreene/2019/07/15/what-can-we-learn-from-an-experimental-high-tech-charter-wunderschool-failure/?sh=5710a334533a

Greene, T. (2020). Let's get explicit. https://learningnuggets.ca/ed-tech-thinks/lets-get-explicit/

Griffiths, S. (2021, August 8). Universities refuse to end online lessons. *The Sunday Times*. https://www.thetimes.co.uk/article/universities-refuse-to-end-online-lessons-h5v3mcmwj

Groom, J. (2008). The glass bees. https://bavatuesdays.com/the-glass-bees/

Groom, J. (2010). EDUPUNK or, on becoming a useful idiot. https://bavatuesdays.com/edupunk-or-on-becoming-a-useful-idiot/

Groom, J. (2017). Let's get small: SPLOTTING the future. http://bavatuesdays.com/lets-get-small-splotting-the-future/

Groom, J. (2018). 25 years of edtech: 2008—EDUPUNK! https://bavatuesdays.com/25-years-of-edtech-2008-edupunk/

Groom, J., & Lamb, B. (2014). Reclaiming innovation. *Educause Review, 49*(3), 29–30.

Growth, A. (2015, July 25). 'Entrepreneurs don't have a special gene for risk—they come from families with money.' *Quartz*. https://qz.com/455109/entrepreneurs-dont-have-a-special-gene-for-risk-they-come-from-families-with-money/

Guest, C. (1848). *The Mabinogion*. https://www.gutenberg.org/files/5160/5160-h/5160-h.htm

Gurven, M., Hill, K., Hames, R., Kameda, T., McDermott, R., Lupo, K., Kiahtipes, C., Ragir, S., & Rosas, A. (2009). Why do men hunt? A reevaluation of "man the hunter" and the sexual division of labor. *Current Anthropology, 50*(1), 51–74.

Hall, R., & Winn, J. (2010, September). The relationships between technology and open education in the development of a resilient higher education. In *Open Education Conference, Barcelona, 2010*. https://core.ac.uk/download/pdf/9627484.pdf

Hamilton, M. (2019). The university is dead, long live the university. *University World News*. https://www.universityworldnews.com/post.php?story=20190211100122511

Harrison, R. (Ed.). (2010). *Understanding the politics of heritage*. Manchester University Press.

Harvey, D. (2018). The outrage economy. https://medium.com/20minutesintothefuture/the-outrage-economy-870a23f65d9c

Helsper, E. J., & Eynon, R. (2010). Digital natives: Where is the evidence? *British Educational Research Journal, 36*(3), 503–520.

Hewison, R. (1987). *The heritage industry: Britain in a climate of decline*. Methuen.

Hiatt, B. (1970). Woman the gatherer. *Australian Aboriginal Studies, 32*, 2–9.

Higginbotham, P. (2012). *Workhouse encyclopedia*. The History Press.

Hill, P. (2020) Revised outlook for higher ed's online response to COVID-19. https://philonedtech.com/revised-outlook-for-higher-eds-online-response-to-covid-19/

Hill, R. (2008). *God's architect: Pugin and the building of romantic Britain*. Yale University Press.

Hilton, J. (2016). Open educational resources and college textbook choices: A review of research on efficacy and perceptions. *Educational Technology Research and Development, 64*(4), 573–590.

Hollands, F. M., & Tirthali, D. (2014). *MOOCs: Expectations and reality. Full report*. Center for Benefit-Cost Studies of Education, Teachers College, Columbia University. https://files.eric.ed.gov/fulltext/ED547237.pdf

Holling, C. S. (1973). Resilience and stability of ecological systems. *Annual Review of Ecology and Systematics, 4*, 1–23.

Holmyard, E. J. (1990). *Alchemy*. Courier Corporation.

HolonIQ. (2020.) 10 charts that explain the global education technology market. https://www.holoniq.com/edtech/10-charts-that-explain-the-global-education-technology-market/

HolonIQ. (2021). OPM + MOOC = OPX. 244 university partnerships in the first half of 2021. https://www.holoniq.com/notes/opm-mooc-opx-244-university-partnerships-in-the-first-half-of-2021/

Hopkins, R. (2009, October 21). Resilience thinking. *Resurgence*. http://transitionculture.org/2009/10/21/resilience-thinking-an-article-for-the-latest-resurgence/

Hotten, R. (2020, November 13). University staff urge probe into e-book pricing "scandal." *BBC News*. https://www.bbc.co.uk/news/business-54922764

Howard, C., Coudriet, C., & Love, K. (2020). 30 under 30: Education. *Forbes* https://www.forbes.com/30-under-30/2020/education/#6f0f071fe6eb

Irvine, V. (2020, October 26). The landscape of merging modalities. *Educause Review*. https://er.educause.edu/articles/2020/10/the-landscape-of-merging-modalities

Jameson, F. (1979). Reification and utopia in mass culture. *Social Text, 1*, 130–148.

Japan Guide. (2001). Newspapers. https://www.japan-guide.com/topic/0108.html

Jenkins, P. (1984). The creation of an "ancient gentry": Glamorgan, 1760–1840. *Welsh History Review/Cylchgrawn Hanes Cymru, 12*, 29.

Jhangiani, R. S., & Jhangiani, S. (2017). Investigating the perceptions, use, and impact of open textbooks: A survey of post-secondary students in British Columbia. *The International Review of Research in Open and Distributed Learning, 18*(4).

Johnson, D. (2020, January 2). How VAR decisions have affected every Premier League club. *ESPN*. https://www.espn.co.uk/football/english-premier-league/story/3929823/how-var-decisions-have-affected-every-premier-league-club

Johnston, D. L. (1978). Scientists become managers—The "T"-shaped man. *IEEE Engineering Management Review, 6*(3), 67–68. https://doi.org/10.1109/emr.1978.4306682

Johnston, E. (2016, November 6). The original "nasty woman." *The Atlantic.* https://www.theatlantic.com/entertainment/archive/2016/11/the-original-nasty-woman-of-classical-myth/506591/

Jones, C., & Shao, B. (2011). *The net generation and digital natives: Implications for higher education.* Higher Education Academy. https://www.advance-he.ac.uk/knowledge-hub/net-generation-and-digital-natives-implications-higher-education

Jordan, K. (2014). Initial trends in enrolment and completion of massive open online courses. *The International Review of Research in Open and Distributed Learning, 15*(1). https://doi.org/10.19173/irrodl.v15i1.1651

Jordan, K. (2017a). Examining the UK higher education sector through the network of institutional accounts on Twitter. *First Monday, 22*(5). http://firstmonday.org/ojs/index.php/fm/article/view/7133/6145. https://doi.org/10.5210/fm.v22i5.7133

Jordan, K. (2017b). *Understanding the structure and role of academics' ego-networks on social networking sites* [PhD dissertation]. The Open University. http://oro.open.ac.uk/48259/

Kamenetz, A. (2010). *DIY U: Edupunks, edupreneurs, and the coming transformation of higher education.* Chelsea Green Publishing.

Kastrenakes, J. (2018, September 13). Jeff Bezos is going to create schools where "the child is the customer." *The Verge.* https://www.theverge.com/2018/9/13/17855358/jeff-bezos-day-one-fund-nonprofit-preschool-amazon

Keats, J. (2008, September 22). Jargon watch: Green crude, popcorning, edupunk. *Wired.* https://www.wired.com/2008/09/st-jw-16/

Kelly, E. (2019). "Big deal" publishing costs European universities over €1B a year. *Science Business.* https://sciencebusiness.net/news/big-deal-publishing-costs-european-universities-over-eu1b-year

Kernohan, D. (2020, August 24). The start of term is not just a problem for universities. *Wonkhe.* https://wonkhe.com/blogs/the-start-of-term-is-not-just-a-problem-for-universities/

Kiley, K. (2011, September 16). Where universities can be cut. *Inside Higher Ed.* https://www.insidehighered.com/news/2011/09/16/where-universities-can-be-cut

Klassen, J. (1990). The disadvantaged and the Hussite revolution. *International Review of Social History, 35*(2), 249–272.

Klein, J. T. (1990). *Interdisciplinarity: History, theory, and practice.* Wayne State University Press.

KNVB. (n.d.). Refereeing 2.0. https://www.knvb.com/themes/new-laws-of-the-game/refereeing-2.0

Kreber, C. (2010). *The university and its disciplines: Teaching and learning within and beyond disciplinary boundaries.* Routledge.

Krishnan, A. (2009). What are academic disciplines? Some observations on the disciplinarity vs. interdisciplinarity debate. *ESRC National Centre for Research Methods NCRM Working Paper Series.* https://eprints.ncrm.ac.uk/id/eprint/783/1/what_are_academic_disciplines.pdf

Kundukulam, V. (2017). Can we Uber-ize education? https://medium.com/@vibink/an-uber-for-education-b4372121a9ad

Lakoff, G. & Johnson, M. (1980). *Metaphors we live by*. University of Chicago Press.

Laporte, C., & Cassuto, L. (2020, April 16). How to responsibly reopen colleges in the fall. *Inside Higher Ed*. https://www.insidehighered.com/views/2020/04/16/practical-advice-how-colleges-can-responsibly-reopen-fall-opinion

Laurillard, D. (2001). *Rethinking university teaching: A conversational framework for the effective use of learning technologies*. Routledge.

Learning Wales. (2018). *Digital competence framework. Hwb*. https://hwb.gov.wales/curriculum-for-wales-2008/digital-competence-framework-curriculum-for-wales-2008-version/

Leckart, S. (2012, March). The Stanford education experiment could change higher learning forever. *Wired*. https://www.wired.com/2012/03/ff_aiclass/

Lee, R. B. (1968). What hunters do for a living, or, how to make out on scarce resources. In R. B. Lee & I. DeVore (Eds.), *Man the hunter* (pp. 30–48). Aldine Publishing Company.

Lee, R. B., & DeVore, I. (Eds.). (1968). *Man the hunter*. Aldine Publishing Company.

Lees, M. (2016, December 1). What Gamergate should have taught us about the "alt-right." *The Guardian*. https://www.theguardian.com/technology/2016/dec/01/gamergate-alt-right-hate-trump

Leiner, B., Cerf, V. G., Clark, D., Kahn, R., Kleinrock, L., Lynch, D., Postel, J., Roberts, L., & Wolff, S. (1997). Brief history of the internet. *The Internet Society*. https://www.internetsociety.org/internet/history-internet/brief-history-internet/

Lessig, L. (2010, October 1). Sorkin vs. Zuckerberg. *The New Republic*. https://newrepublic.com/article/78081/sorkin-zuckerberg-the-social-network

Levi, P. (1986). *The Drowned and the Saved*. Abacus.

Levy, S. (2019, September 18). Richard Stallman and the fall of the clueless nerd. *Wired*. https://www.wired.com/story/richard-stallman-and-the-fall-of-the-clueless-nerd/

Lewin, D. (2013, December 11). After setbacks, online courses are re-thought. *New York Times*. https://www.nytimes.com/2013/12/11/us/after-setbacks-online-courses-are-rethought.html?_r=0

Lovejoy, C. O. (1981). The origin of man. *Science, 211*(4480), 341–350.

Loveless, N. (2019). *How to make art at the end of the world: A manifesto for research-creation*. Duke University Press.

Lowe, S., Browne, M., Boudjelas, S., & De Poorter, M. (2000). *100 of the world's worst invasive alien species: A selection from the global invasive species database*. The Invasive Species Specialist Group, a Specialist Group of the Species Survival Commission of the World Conservation Union. http://www.issg.org/pdf/publications/worst_100/english_100_worst.pdf

Lukeš, D. (2019, May). Explanation is an event, understanding is a process: How (not) to explain anything with metaphor. *Metaphor Hacker*. https://metaphorhacker

.net/2019/05/explanation-is-an-event-understanding-is-a-process-how-not-to
-explain-anything-with-metaphor/

Mackness, J., & Bell, F. (2015). Rhizo14: A rhizomatic learning cMOOC in sunlight and in shade. *Open Praxis, 7*(1), 25–38.

Maiklem, L. (2019). *Mudlarking: Lost and found on the river Thames.* Bloomsbury.

Martínez, M. A., Sauleda, N., & Huber, G. L. (2001). Metaphors as blueprints of thinking about teaching and learning. *Teaching and Teacher Education, 17*(8), 965–977.

Masnick, M. (2005, January 5). Since when is it illegal to just mention a trademark online? *Techdirt.* https://www.techdirt.com/articles/20050105/0132239.shtml

Mason, L. (2018). A critical metaphor analysis of educational technology research in the social studies. *Contemporary Issues in Technology and Teacher Education, 18*(3), 538–555.

Mason, R. (2005). Nation building at the Museum of Welsh Life. *Museum and Society, 3*(1), 18–34.

McAndrew, P., & Scanlon, E. (2013). Open learning at a distance: Lessons for struggling MOOCs. *Science, 342*(6165), 1450–1451.

McBride, S. (2019, September 4). Uber's nightmare has just begun. *Forbes.* https://www.forbes.com/sites/stephenmcbride1/2019/09/04/ubers-nightmare-has-just-started/#521f5859b7e0

McCloskey, D. N. (2005). Storytelling in economics. In C. Nash (Ed.), *Narrative in culture: The uses of storytelling in the sciences, philosophy and literature* (pp. 21–38). Routledge.

McKeever, M. (2019). *Emperors of the deep: The ocean's most mysterious, misunderstood and important guardians.* Harper.

McLees, D. (2005). *Castell Coch* (Revised ed.). Cadw.

Mead, G. (1934). *Mind, self and society.* University of Chicago Press.

Medeiros, J. (2018, June 23). The inside story of how FIFA's controversial VAR system was born. *Wired.* https://www.wired.co.uk/article/var-football-world-cup

Microsoft. (2021). *What's new in Microsoft Education.* https://www.microsoft.com/en-gb/education

Mitra, S. (2005). Self organising systems for mass computer literacy: Findings from the "hole in the wall" experiments. *International Journal of Development Issues, 4*(1), 71–81.

Monbiot, G. (2013, May 27). My manifesto for rewilding the world. *The Guardian.* https://www.theguardian.com/commentisfree/2013/may/27/my-manifesto-rewilding-world

Morris, N. P., Swinnerton, B., & Coop, T. (2019). Lecture recordings to support learning: A contested space between students and teachers. *Computers & Education, 140,* https://doi.org/10.1016/j.compedu.2019.103604

Muscatelli, A. (2020, January 15). Universities must overhaul the toxic working culture for academic researchers. *The Guardian.* https://www.theguardian.com/

education/2020/jan/15/universities-must-overhaul-the-toxic-working-culture
-for-academic-researchers

Nardi, B. A., & O'Day, V. (2000). *Information ecologies: Using technology with heart*. MIT Press.

Naughton, J. (1999). *A brief history of the future: Origins of the internet*. Weidenfeld & Nicolson.

Naughton, J. (2011). *From Gutenberg to Zuckerberg: What you really need to know about the internet*. Quercus Publishing.

Nead, N. (2019). The education technology (edtech) industry: Overview of mergers, acquisitions and venture capital trends & investments. *Investment Bank*. https://investmentbank.com/edtech-industry/

Neilan, C. (2021, August 10). Resume face-to-face lectures or cut fees, education secretary tells universities. *The Daily Telegraph*. https://www.telegraph.co.uk/politics/2021/08/10/resume-face-to-face-lectures-cut-fees-education-secretary-tells/

Oblinger, D., & Oblinger, J. (2005). Is it age or IT: First steps toward understanding the net generation. *Educating the Net Generation*, Educause. https://www.educause.edu/research-and-publications/books/educating-net-generation/it-age-or-it-first-steps-toward-understanding-net-generation

OpenLearn. (2020). *OpenLearn annual report 2019–20*. http://www.open.ac.uk/business/sites/www.open.ac.uk.business/files/files/OpenLearn%202019-20%20Annual%20Report%20EXTERNAL.pdf

Orange, H. (2008). Industrial archaeology: Its place within the academic discipline, the public realm and the heritage industry. *Industrial Archaeology Review, 30*(2), 83–95.

Oravec, J. A. (2003). Blending by blogging: Weblogs in blended learning initiatives. *Journal of Educational Media, 28*(2–3), 225–233.

Oskam, I. F. (2009). T-shaped engineers for interdisciplinary innovation: An attractive perspective for young people as well as a must for innovative organisations. In *37th Annual Conference—Attracting Students in Engineering*, Rotterdam, The Netherlands (Vol. 14).

Oxford English Dictionary. (2021). Evangelist.

Paine, A. (2020). Online radio listening up during lockdown—but no RAJAR figures for Q2. *MusicWeek*. https://www.musicweek.com/media/read/online-radio-listening-up-during-lockdown-but-no-rajar-figures-for-q2/080604

Palfreyman, D., & Farrington, D. (2020, October 30). Can students get a discount on their fees this year? *Wonkhe*. https://wonkhe.com/blogs/can-students-get-a-discount-on-their-fees-this-year/

Paltiel, A. D., Zheng, A., & Walensky, R. P. (2020). COVID-19 screening strategies that permit the safe re-opening of college campuses. *medRxiv*. https://doi.org/10.1101/2020.07.06.20147702

Pappano, L. (2012, November 11). The year of the MOOC. *New York Times*. https://www.nytimes.com/2012/11/04/education/edlife/massive-open-online-courses-are-multiplying-at-a-rapid-pace.html

Parr, S. (2012, March 30). We know our education system is broken, so why can't we fix it? *FastCompany.* https://www.fastcompany.com/1826287/we-know-our-education-system-broken-so-why-cant-we-fix-it

Perna, L. W., Ruby, A., Boruch, R. F., Wang, N., Scull, J., Ahmad, S., & Evans, C. (2014). Moving through MOOCs: Understanding the progression of users in massive open online courses. *Educational Researcher, 43*(9), 421–432.

Perry, W. (1976). *Open University: A personal account by the first vice-chancellor.* Open University Press.

Pickard, L. (2018). TU Delft students can earn credit for MOOCs from other universities. *Class Central.* https://www.class-central.com/report/delft-virtual-exchange-program/

Prensky, M. (2001). Digital natives, digital immigrants part 1. *On the Horizon, 9*(5), 1–6.

Prensky, M. (2011). Digital wisdom and homo sapiens digital. In M. Thomas (Ed.), *Deconstructing digital natives: Young people, technology and the new literacies* (pp. 15–29). Taylor and Francis.

Prensky, M. (2016). *Education to better their world: Unleashing the power of 21st-century kids.* Teachers College Press.

Preston-Whyte, R. (2004). The beach as a liminal space. In A. A. Lew, C. M. Hall, & A. M. Williams (Eds.), *A companion to tourism.* (pp. 349–359). John Wiley & Sons.

Price, E. G., & Iber, J. (2006). *Hip hop culture.* ABC-CLIO.

Purdy, J. P., & Walker, J. R. (2013). Liminal spaces and research identity: The construction of introductory composition students as researchers. *Pedagogy, 13*(1), 9–41.

Railway Intelligence. (1846, February 28). *Cardiff and Merthyr Guardian, Glamorgan, Monmouth, and Brecon Gazette.* http://papuraunewyddcymru.llgc.org.uk/en/page/view/3088647/ART30/

Raths, D. (2016, September 19). Why it's time for education technology to become an academic discipline. *Campus Technology.* https://campustechnology.com/articles/2016/09/19/why-its-time-for-education-technology-to-become-an-academic-discipline.aspx?admgarea=News

Rayment-Pickard, H. (2020, April 15). Digital can't replace face to face when it comes to widening participation. *Wonkhe.* https://wonkhe.com/blogs/digital-cant-replace-face-to-face-when-it-comes-to-widening-participation/

Rigg, P. (2014). Can universities survive the digital age? *University World News.* https://www.universityworldnews.com/post.php?story=20141030125107100

Ris, E. W. (2015). Grit: A short history of a useful concept. *Journal of Educational Controversy, 10*(1), Article 3. https://cedar.wwu.edu/jec/vol10/iss1/3

Robinson, M. (2017, June 14). Billionaires are stockpiling land that could be used in the apocalypse—Here's where they're going. *Business Insider.* https://www.businessinsider.com/billionaire-doomsday-preppers-escape-plans-2017-6?r=UK

Rogers, G. (2014). The Uberization of education. https://www.linkedin.com/pulse/20140603135511-20348008-the-uberization-of-education/

Rowe, A. (2019, June 25). 6 facts about the $26 billion that U.S. publishers earned in 2018. *Forbes*. https://www.forbes.com/sites/adamrowe1/2019/06/25/6-facts-about-the-26-billion-that-us-publishers-earned-in-2018/?sh=328e06627e61

Rubey, D. (1976). The *Jaws* in the mirror. *Jump Cut, 10–11*, 20–23. https://www.ejumpcut.org/archive/onlinessays/JC10-11folder/JawsRubey.html

Ruth, S. (2014, July). Can MOOCs help reduce college tuition? MOOCs and technology to advance learning and learning research (Ubiquity symposium). *Ubiquity*, 1–10. https://dl.acm.org/doi/pdf/10.1145/2591685

Saini, A. (2017). *Inferior: How science got women wrong and the new research that's rewriting the story*. Beacon Press.

Sanford, K., Merkel, L., & Madill, L. (2011). "There's no fixed course": Rhizomatic learning communities in adolescent videogaming. *Loading . . . The Journal of the Canadian Game Studies Association, 5*(8), 50–70.

Schön, D. A. (1993). Generative metaphor: A perspective on problem-setting in social policy. In A. Ortony (Ed.), *Metaphor and thought* (pp. 137–163). Cambridge University Press.

Seldon, A., & Abidoye, O. (2018). *The fourth education revolution*. Legend Press.

Selwyn, N. (2015). Data entry: Towards the critical study of digital data and education. *Learning, Media and Technology, 40*(1), 64–82.

Sfard, A. (1998). On two metaphors for learning and the dangers of choosing just one. *Educational Researcher, 27*(2), 4–13.

Shirky, C. (2008) *Here comes everybody: The power of organizing without organizations*. Allen Lane.

Shirky, C. (2012, December 17). Higher education: Our MP3 is the MOOC. *The Guardian*. https://www.theguardian.com/education/2012/dec/17/moocs-higher-education-transformation

Siemens, G. (2005). Connectivism: A learning theory for the digital age. https://jotamac.typepad.com/jotamacs_weblog/files/Connectivism.pdf

Siemens, G. (2013). Learning analytics: The emergence of a discipline. *American Behavioral Scientist, 57*(10), 1380–1400.

Singh, S. (2015). The fallacy of open. In M. Bali, C. Cronin, L. Czerniewicz, R. DeRosa, & R. Jhangiani (Eds.), *Open at the margins: Critical perspectives on open education* (pp. 23–38). Rebus Press.

Singler, B. (2017, June 13). fAIth. *Aeon*. https://aeon.co/essays/why-is-the-language-of-transhumanists-and-religion-so-similar

Slocum, S. (1975). Women the gatherer: Male bias in anthropology. In R. Reiter (Ed.), *Toward an anthropology of women* (pp 36–50). Monthly Review Press.

Smith, D. W., & Bangs, E. E. (2009). Reintroduction of wolves to Yellowstone National Park: History, values, and ecosystem restoration. In M. W. Hayward & M. Somers (Eds.) *Reintroduction of top-order predators* (pp. 92–125). Wiley-Blackwell.

Smith, L. (2006). *Uses of heritage*. Routledge.

Smooke, D. (2018). Building to be the Airbnb of international education. *Hacker-noon*. https://hackernoon.com/building-to-be-the-airbnb-of-international-education-3b0d39c75b21

Snow, D. (2001). *Collective identity and expressive forms*. Center for the Study of Democracy. http://escholarship.org/uc/item/2zn1t7bj

SPLOT. (2021). https://splot.ca/

Sterling, K. (2014). Man the hunter, woman the gatherer? The impact of gender studies on hunter-gatherer research (a retrospective). In V. Cummings, P. Jordan, & M. Zvelebil (Eds.), *The Oxford handbook of the archaeology and anthropology of hunter-gatherers* (151). Oxford University Press.

Stewart, B. (2016). Collapsed publics: Orality, literacy, and vulnerability in academic Twitter. *Journal of Applied Social Theory, 1*(1). https://socialtheoryapplied.com/journal/jast/article/view/33/9

Stone, Z. (2017, March 20). Why millennials are obsessed with the apocalypse. *Forbes*. https://www.forbes.com/sites/zarastone/2017/03/20/why-millennials-are-obsessed-with-the-apocalypse/

Suchman, L. A. (1987). *Plans and situated actions: The problem of human-machine communication*. Cambridge University Press.

Supiano, B. (2020, May 28). Can you create learning communities online? *The Chronicle of Higher Education*. https://www.chronicle.com/newsletter/teaching/2020-05-28

Tapscott, D. (1998). *Growing up digital: The rise of the net generation*. McGraw-Hill.

Theus, M., & Interkom, V. I. A. G. (1999). User interfaces of interactive statistical graphics software. *Computing Science and Statistics*, 123–129.

Thibodeau, P., McClelland, J. L., & Boroditsky, L. (2009). When a bad metaphor may not be a victimless crime: The role of metaphor in social policy. In N. A. Taatgen, & H. van Rijn. *Proceedings of the 31st Annual Conference of the Cognitive Science Society* (Vol. 29, pp. 809–814). Cognitive Science Society.

Topham, G. (2019, November 25). Uber loses London licence after TfL finds drivers faked identity. *The Guardian*. https://www.theguardian.com/technology/2019/nov/25/uber-loses-licence-london-tfl

Tree, I. (2018). *Wilding: The return of nature to a British farm*. Macmillan.

Turner, V. (1969). *The ritual process: Structure and anti-structure*. Routledge.

UNESCO. (2016). 263 million children and youth are out of school. http://uis.unesco.org/en/news/263-million-children-and-youth-are-out-school

UNESCO. (2020). Education: From disruption to recovery. https://en.unesco.org/covid19/educationresponse

Unger, R., and Warfel, T. (2011, February 15). Getting guerrilla with it. *UX Magazine*, Article 620. http://uxmag.com/articles/getting-guerrilla-with-it

Van Gennep, A. (1960). *The rites of passage*. Routledge.

Vasant, S., Nerantzi, C., Beckingham, S., Lewin-Jones, J., Sellers, R., Turner, S., & Withnell, N. (2018). LTHEchat—The story of a community of practice through

Twitter. *Association for Learning Technology Blog*. https://altc.alt.ac.uk/blog/ 2018/02/lthechat-the-story-of-a-community-of-practice-through-twitter/#gref

Vassari, G. (1550). *The lives of the artists*. Oxford University Press.

Vaughan-Nichols, S. (2015, November 11). How bad a boss is Linus Torvalds? *Computer World*. https://www.computerworld.com/article/3004387/how-bad-a -boss-is-linus-torvalds.html

Veletsianos, G. (2019, May 27). In education, what can be made more flexible? https://www.veletsianos.com/2019/05/27/what-can-be-made-more-flexible -in-education/

Veletsianos, G. (2021, July 24). *Twitter*. https://twitter.com/veletsianos/status/ 1419031265181798400

Veletsianos, G., & Shepherdson, P. (2016). A systematic analysis and synthesis of the empirical MOOC literature published in 2013–2015. *International Review of Research in Open and Distributed Learning, 17*(2), 198–221.

Vermeulen, E. (2019). Education is broken in an age of human technology. *The StartUp*. https://medium.com/swlh/education-is-broken-in-an-age-of-human -technology-7891085e7252

Waite, M., Mackness, J., Roberts, G., & Lovegrove, E. (2013). Liminal participants and skilled orienteers: Learner participation in a MOOC for new lecturers. *Journal of Online Learning and Teaching, 9*(2), 200–215.

Wakefield, A., Cartney, P., Christie, J., Smyth, R., Cooke, A., Jones, T., & Kennedy, J. (2018). Do MOOCs encourage corporate social responsibility or are they simply a marketing opportunity? *Nurse Education in Practice, 33*, 37–41.

Walker, B., Holling, C. S., Carpenter, S. R., & Kinzig, A. (2004). Resilience, adaptability and transformability in social-ecological systems. *Ecology and Society, 9*(2), Article 5. http://www.ecologyandsociety.org/vol9/iss2/art5

Wang, A. (2017, June 6). Mark Zuckerberg's dream for education is for kids to learn mostly without teachers. *Quartz*. https://qz.com/999735/facebook-ceo-mark -zuckerbergs-plan-for-education-is-kids-teaching-themselves-and-teachers -helping/

Washburn, S., & Lancaster, C. (1968). The evolution of hunting. In R. Lee & I. DeVore (Eds.), *Man the hunter* (pp. 293–303). Aldine.

Watters, A. (2013a). Zombie ideas (ed-tech ideas that refuse to die, even though we know they're monstrous). http://2013trends.hackeducation.com/zombies.html

Watters, A. (2013b, June 24). The myth and the millennialism of "disruptive innovation." http://hackeducation.com/2013/05/24/disruptive-innovation

Watters, A. (2015) The invented history of 'the factory model of education.' http://hackeducation.com/2015/04/25/factory-model

Watters, A. (2016, September 9). Re·con·figures: The pigeons of ed-tech. http:// hackeducation.com/2016/09/22/pigeon

Watters, A. (2019, December 31). The 100 worst ed-tech debacles of the decade. http://hackeducation.com/2019/12/31/what-a-shitshow

Weale, S. (2019, September 27). Top of the class: Labour seeks to emulate Finland's school system. *The Guardian.* https://www.theguardian.com/education/2019/sep/27/top-class-finland-schools-envy-world-ofsted-education

Weller, M. (2007). Educator as DJ. http://blog.edtechie.net/web-2-0/educator_as_dj/

Weller, M. (2011). *The digital scholar: How technology is transforming scholarly practice.* Bloomsbury Academic. https://doi.org/10.5040/9781849666275

Weller, M. (2014). *Battle for open: How openness won and why it doesn't feel like victory.* Ubiquity Press.

Weller, M. (2016). Ed tech as discipline. http://blog.edtechie.net/edtech/ed-tech-as-dsicipline/

Weller, M. (2020). *25 years of ed tech.* Athabasca University Press.

Weller, M., & Anderson, T. (2013). Digital resilience in higher education. *European Journal of Open, Distance and e-Learning, 16*(1), 53.

West, S. (2012). The English landscape garden 1680–1760. In E. Barker (Ed.), *Art & visual culture 1600–1850: Academy to avant-garde.* Tate Publishing.

Whitchurch, C. (2008). Shifting identities and blurring boundaries: The emergence of third space professionals in UK higher education. *Higher Education Quarterly, 62*(4), 377–396.

Wikipedia. (2016). Digital scholarship. https://en.wikipedia.org/wiki/Digital_scholarship

Wikipedia. (2021). Mudlark. https://en.wikipedia.org/wiki/Mudlark

Wiley, D. (2005, December 28). Teacher as DJ. https://opencontent.org/blog/archives/227

Williams, D. (1955). *The Rebecca riots: A study in agrarian discontent.* University of Wales Press.

Williams, D. (1959). Chartism in Wales. In A, Briggs (ed.) *Chartist Studies*, 220–48. Macmillan.

Williamson, B. (2017). Educating Silicon Valley: Corporate education reform and the reproduction of the techno-economic revolution. *Review of Education, Pedagogy, and Cultural Studies, 39*(3), 265–288.

Williamson, T. (2007). Archaeological perspectives on landed estates: Research agendas. In J. Finch & K. Giles (Eds.), *Estate landscapes: Design, improvement and power in the post-medieval landscape* (pp. 1–18). Woodbridge.

Willingham, D. T., Hughes, E. M., & Dobolyi, D. G. (2015). The scientific status of learning styles theories. *Teaching of Psychology, 42*(3), 266–271.

Wilson, B. G. (1995). Metaphors for instruction: Why we talk about learning environments. *Educational Technology, 35*(5), 25–30.

Wilson, P. L., Bamford, C., & Townley, K. (2007). *Green hermeticism: Alchemy and ecology.* Steiner Books.

Wolfson, L. (2013, June 18). Venture capital needed for "broken" U.S. education, Thrun says. *Bloomberg Business Week.* http://www.businessweek.com/news/2013-06-18/venture-capital-needed-for-broken-u-dot-s-dot-education-thrun-says

Wong, J. C. (2019, April 11). Disgruntled drivers and "cultural challenges": Uber admits to its biggest risk factors. *The Guardian*. https://www.theguardian.com/technology/2019/apr/11/uber-ipo-risk-factors

Wood, P. (2012). Blogs as liminal space: Student teachers at the threshold. *Technology, Pedagogy and Education, 21*(1), 85–99.

Wright, P. (1985). *On living in an old country*. Oxford University Press.

Xu, H., & Ruef, M. (2004). The myth of the risk-tolerant entrepreneur. *Strategic Organization, 2*(4), 331–355.

Zihlman, A. L. (1978). Women in evolution, part II: Subsistence and social organization among early hominids. *Signs: Journal of Women in Culture and Society, 4*(1), 4–20.

Zimmerman, J. (2020). Video kills the teaching star. *The Chronicle of Higher Education*. https://www.chronicle.com/article/video-kills-the-teaching-star/

ABOUT THE AUTHOR

MARTIN WELLER is professor of educational technology, in the Institute of Educational Technology at the UK Open University. He is the chair of the Open University's multidisciplinary degree, the Open Programme, which is the largest degree in the UK. He is the author of *The Battle for Open* (2014), *The Digital Scholar* (2011), and *25 Years of Ed Tech* (2020).